the CULTURE WAR

The Culture War

Jonathon Van Maren

Life Cycle Books
Toronto, Ontario • Fort Collins, Colorado

ISBN: 978-0-919225-49-7

Design by: Aimée Rochard

Cover design by: Gerrit van Dorland

Published & distributed by Life Cycle Books
www.lifecyclebooks.com orders@lifecyclebooks.com

Printed in Canada

To my beautiful Charmaine,
a wonderful wife and ruthless editor,

&

to the two people I will never run out of things to thank for,
Mom and Dad

Contents

Foreword

The value of this book, for those of us now departing what the old Anglican liturgy calls "this fleeting world," is hard to overstate. It describes a convulsive revolution that we watched happen around us over the last fifty or so years. The operative word here is "watched." For though it undermined and largely destroyed some of the most hallowed and critically essential principles upon which our whole society is founded, the appalling truth is that few in my generation (I'm now 87) did anything substantial to resist it.

Yes, we questioned, whined, wondered and occasionally deplored what we saw happening, but the revolutionaries scoffed. They knew we would not man the barricades to defend the old order, bequeathed to us by our ancestors and paid for over many generations with a great deal of blood. And they were right. They won because we let them win.

But it seemed to happen so suddenly. One day we woke up to discover the world had astonishingly changed. Sexual strictures we had once considered unshakeable had been shaken out of existence. Deeds once prohibited by the criminal code had now become not just legal, but unassailable. Sacred, one might say, insofar as anything remained sacred.

To even criticize the new lifestyles and "freedoms" had become an act of "hate," punishable by fine or imprisonment. Meanwhile, the authority of the family was gradually being usurped by the state. In many jurisdictions, for example, parents caught spanking their children, something parents have been doing since the dawn of humanity, were now subject to criminal prosecution. The public school system, once a strong bulwark of support for faith and family, now worked diligently to undermine both. The old "values" must go; the child must become more "advanced" than the parent. Such was officialdom's thinking.

And who were these revolutionaries? The brute fact is that they were our own children, many of them now in their sixties and accurately described as "the Boomers"—accurately, because in the main they have lived their entire lives in boom times. In fact, they were the most affluent, comfortable, economically secure, physically healthy, and painless society yet known to man. They are also the most pampered, under-challenged, and over-valued generation, which has largely paid its way on borrowed government money. Its unfortunate heirs and descendants will somehow have to pay it back.

Being a member of these ill-starred heirs of the Boomers, Van Maren is understandably aggrieved at what they have done to our society. He depicts it in clinical detail—the abortion business, the baby body-parts business, the porn business, the sex slave business, the gradually establishing euthanasia business. He doesn't go into the business of drugs and drug-related crime, another endowment to humanity bestowed upon us by the Boomers. But everything else is here, phase by phase, horror by horror, as it transpired year by year, decade by decade.

Many will find it an uneasy book to read. He knows this. But he also knows how our reluctance to face reality led to our defeat. As each new outrage succeeded the former outrage, we soon became inured to outrage itself. We found ourselves quietly acquiescing to forms of behaviour we would once have regarded as utterly abominable, even unmentionable. So we gave up reading about it and let things happen. But Van Maren won't let us get away with this. In effect, he is saying: *Like it or not, to ignore these things is to accept them.* So yes, read it. Become disgusted, sickened, and then act.

But act how? Is the war not over? Is it not already lost? He certainly does not think so. But he also warns that before it gets better it may well become worse, that the present attack on Christian morality will soon become a war against Christianity itself. However, of two further realities he is himself both aware and at work.

First, he knows that their history will not be written by the Boomers, but by his own generation. And they, burdened as they will be by the inevitable consequences of the assorted insanities heaped upon them by their forebears, will not see the Boomers as they see themselves--founders of a shining era of new liberties, rights, tolerance, reason and "choice." Instead, what they will see is a squalid return to animal barbarism and the dominance of "me" over every thing and everybody else, all being paid for by the luckless lot they left behind. This book, that is, may well be a forerunner of a great many more that take up the same theme. That makes it a must-read for many people.

Second, he realizes that the winner of the Culture War will not be determined by judges, politicians and academics, but by the workings of what the Christians call "judgment." That is, by the natural consequences of the changes made. If they turn out good, they will help create a better society. If they turn out bad, they will destroy the society we have. As this book so graphically discloses, all the results to date are in the negative. Our enemies, the revolutionaries, do not appear to realize this. They have deluded themselves into thinking that now that officialdom has spoken, all will be well. They're wrong, and as we see things crumbling around us, we should be sure to call this to their attention. Van Maren certainly has.

TED BYFIELD
EDMONTON, ALBERTA
JUNE 28, 2016

Introduction

There is the moral of all human tales;
'Tis but the same rehearsal of the past,
First freedom, then glory—when that fails,
Wealth, vice, corruption—barbarism at last,
And history, with all her volumes vast,
Hath but one page.

—Lord Byron

I was raised in a Christian home. If you had asked me when I was growing up if I was pro-life, I would have told you that I most certainly was. I might even have told you that abortion was murder. But I would not have been able to tell you *why* this was the case. I certainly hadn't ever conceptualized the country I lived in as one that endorsed and facilitated the killing of millions of children. In fact, when one of my high school teachers gave my class an essay to read on the "progressive" war on the family, I scoffed. War on the family? How very dramatic.

In my first year of university, one of my professors brought up abortion. He didn't make the case for it, because he clearly felt that he didn't need to. He merely referred to it as one of the many social goods our enlightened society permits—and in Canada's case, pays for—in the 21st century. Feeling unsettled, I headed to the library on my lunch break, Googled the word "abortion," and clicked on a video. The next three minutes changed everything for me, as I watched a baby literally get pulled apart with sharp metal tools. I felt physically sick.

I joined the pro-life club on campus and began giving presentations on abortion. We hosted abortion debates, set up educational displays, and debated our peers. Angry protestors trashed many of our displays. In 2010, when I completed my history degree, I made the decision to work in the pro-life movement full-time, and joined the Canadian Centre for Bio-

Ethical Reform. Debating hundreds of people on campuses, street corners, and elsewhere, I began to realize how broken our culture was. Our twisted view of sexuality, the pathetic state of the institution of marriage, pandemic rates of porn use, increasing levels of sexual assault, and a depressing view of the value of human life have created a society filled with hurting, angry people.

To understand how we got to where we are and how our broken culture had been snapped in so many different places, I began to research. I spoke with students about their experiences, and then searched through sociological studies to find trends. I tried to find correlations between different sets of statistics. I read scores of history books, trying to piece together a cultural narrative that would explain the present state of affairs. What follows in these pages is the result of my attempt to make sense of everything.

I should perhaps first explain what I am *not* trying to accomplish. I am not trying to write an apologetics book. Others have already written many books filled with brilliant arguments to equip Christians in defending their worldview, and I refer to many of them in the footnotes throughout this book in hopes that some will find their interest piqued and will read those books as well. What I have tried to do here is part historical analysis and part cultural analysis, with many of my own experiences woven in throughout. Above all, I want to give people a readable narrative so that they can better understand the situation we find ourselves in. People who are disinclined to pick up thick history books and academic analyses, I hope, will find this book more engaging.

Too often, we look at different battles in the culture war as if they are disconnected. Hook-up culture, pornography, abortion, euthanasia, rape culture, and the decline of marriage—they are all connected. Some connections are obvious, such as hook-up culture creating a demand for abortion. Other connections, such as those between abortion and pornography, may be more difficult to discern at first glance. My hope is that upon completing this book, the reader will have a conceptualization of where our culture is at—and how we got here.

The reality that underlies the entire culture war, of course, is the fact that the West has rejected Christianity, and with it the moral framework our culture rested upon for generations. In Canada, while many still claim to be nominally religious and may adopt a religious label as a nod to their culture or heritage, they have still been abandoning the churches in droves. "The percentage of the Canadian population attending religious services on a regular basis," reported Statistics Canada in 2008, "has declined over the past 20 years. According to the General Social Survey (GSS), 21% of Canadians aged 15 and over reported they attended a religious service at least once a week in 2005, down from 30% in 1985."[1]

A similar situation prevails in the United States. "According to the Hartford Institute of Religion Research," writes Toni Ridgeway, "more than 40 percent of people say they go to church every week, but statistics show that fewer than 20 percent actually attend. More than 4,000 churches close their doors every year. Between 2010 and 2012, half of all churches in the U.S. did not add any new members. Each year 2.7 million church members fall into inactivity."[2]

As those of us in the pro-life movement have found out, there is no guarantee that those who attend church have any real belief in what Christianity has to say on the most important cultural issues of our day. We meet many who support abortion, or at least refuse to condemn it. Increasing numbers support the redefinition of marriage. And this is to say nothing of a trend referred to by culture-watchers as "sexual atheism," which indicates the skyrocketing numbers of young churchgoers who claim to believe everything found in the Apostle's Creed, but don't think that the Christian view of sexuality has any relevance for them.

If I were to include an entire history of the decline of Christian faith across the Western world, this book would double, if not triple in size. That would defeat my intention of providing people with a readable cultural narrative, and so I will avoid doing so. It is simply necessary to acknowledge that our current cultural winds are beating down upon a society built on a foundation of sand. We have forgotten that God is the Author and Creator of all things. Our countries have forgotten their own heritage. The Peace Tower of the Canadian Parliament buildings bears an inscription of Proverbs 29:18: "Where there is no vision, the people perish: but he that keepeth the law, happy is he." The signers of the American Declaration of Independence recognized, from the very beginning, that all rights came from "the Creator." We have forgotten these truths at our peril.

What follows is a history, an analysis, and an autopsy. I hope it may prove useful.

Chapter 1

The Forgotten and Misunderstood History of the Sexual Revolution

The 1970s blew to smithereens an entire structure of sexual morality. Revolutions like that do not last forever. They cannot. But the ending of a revolution is not the same thing as the restoration of the old order. It is the institutionalization of a new one.

—David Frum, *How We Got Here*

The Sexual Revolution and the new normal

There is no series of historical events that has impacted every human living in the Western world today—and even beyond—more than the Sexual Revolution. And yet, while many are certainly familiar with the term, almost no one can explain what the Sexual Revolution is. Internet pornography, legalized abortion, the gay liberation movement, hook-up culture, contraception, public nudity, transgenderism, and threats to religious freedom are all either part of or the direct result of the Sexual Revolution. Television, the film industry, advertising agencies, academia, the media, and the music industry have all been shaped by the Sexual Revolution, and play an incessantly active role in promoting it. We are so saturated by these influences that rarely do we even notice. We simply take it for granted that this is the way things are, often without questioning how or why these things came to be.

For example, consider hook-up culture on campuses, now considered the norm and lionized in dozens of stupid campus comedy films. When I was attending Simon Fraser University in British Columbia, Canada, it was accepted that the binge-drinking that took place was being accompanied by casual sex—and if that wasn't happening, it wasn't for lack of effort on behalf of the students. There was even a "Campus Hook-Up Bingo" game in the student newspaper, featuring great places to have sex like the baseball diamond and the lecture halls. One student had reportedly managed to convince someone to have casual coitus with him in every one of these locations.

I had discussions about campus hook-up culture often. One friend demanded to know why I wasn't sleeping around. I responded with a question: "How many of the people that you were with do you wish you hadn't hooked up with?" After a pause, the thoughtful response: "Most of them, I guess. Maybe even all of them." Another classmate demanded to know how I could call myself a "dude" if I wasn't "sleeping with chicks." I simply asked him whether it took more of a man to keep one woman happy for a life time or dozens for ten minutes. To that one, I got an arched eyebrow, an appreciative chuckle, and no follow-up questioning.

The thing that shocked me? Almost none of them had considered the idea that perhaps waiting to have sex with someone you loved, inside of marriage, was worth it. Not one. Hook-up culture is the new normal. It is Christian sexual ethics that are the counter-culture. And it is imperative that we understand what happened to make it so.

As I travel across North America speaking on abortion and pornography, one of the things I often hear is a hopelessness and despair that the West is being flattened by the juggernaut of spreading moral decay. There is a feeling among many people that the restriction of religious liberty, the continued legality of abortion, and the redefinition of marriage are inevitable.

This is, of course, one of the most prominent and successful strategies of the secular left—they create an aura of inevitability while concurrently demonizing all those who oppose this new and mangled "progress" as Neanderthals on the cusp of being left behind by history. That inevitability becomes a self-fulfilling prophecy, because many people don't realize that the various battles in the Sexual Revolution actually all correlate to one another—that what we are seeing now is the end game of an incredibly vast and well-planned cultural project.

Forgotten history

To understand the Sexual Revolution, it is essential to first understand the academic underpinnings that paved the way for the massive social change that swept the West during the 1960s and beyond. And the fact is that almost nothing you've heard or been taught is true. History has been presented to us in a deliberately false way. As George Orwell once noted, "The most effective way to destroy people is to deny and obliterate their own understanding of their history."

In today's culture, knowledge of history is itself fast becoming history. Late-night hosts have been known to make comedic hay of this growing cultural Alzheimer's by asking people in the street mundane questions such as "Who were our allies in World War II?" to hilariously cringe-worthy responses.

But there is a distinctly unfunny side to our forgetfulness. We are very much at risk, as the old saying goes, not just of repeating history because we have forgotten it, but of repeating it without even being aware that we are repeating it. It was this point that veteran Canadian journalist and author Ted Byfield, now in his eighties, emphasized over and over when I spoke with him some time ago. "We are swiftly abandoning many of the fundamental social and moral principles upon which our civilization is based," he said. "That is, we're zealously cutting off the branch we're sitting on...very few people, whether educated or uneducated, know where those principles came from, and how we came to embrace them. We are dangerously ignorant of our own heritage and history."*

---

* Ted Byfield was for decades the voice of social conservatism in Canada, with his magazines *The Alberta Report* and *The BC Report* as well as many books detailing his opposition to the decline of Christian values in society at large. Influential in both journalism and politics, he could best be described as Canada's William F. Buckley.

Byfield is right. When I began researching the social history of the West several years ago, I found myself consistently stunned by the simple fact that much of what I'd been taught—or at least led to believe—was untrue. While many university professors are lovely teachers and impressive academics that I count myself privileged to have met, there are also many aging hippies who abandoned their communes after the first good rainstorm for a more fertile way of disseminating their ideology—academia. In lecture halls in front of thousands of students, they sell their own version of how history has unfolded, leaving most of us completely unaware of how things have actually happened.

I've thought of this often since completing my own degree in history—Christian parents struggle against the influences of the culture to inculcate their children with traditional values and a Christian worldview, and then often pony up tens of thousands of dollars to universities just to give their faculties four years to dissuade them of this worldview.

This has often created in Christian parents a despair as they see their children drift farther and farther from their beliefs, heritage, and worldview—and these parents are often not equipped with the arguments to explain how their children are being sold a false bill of goods.

And they are. Consider, for example, a woman who could quite accurately be called "The Mother of the Sexual Revolution."

MARGARET MEAD AND THE 1928 *COMING OF AGE IN SAMOA*

Margaret Mead was a young anthropologist with a set of very specific ideological goals. She set out to help anthropology professor Frank Boas of Columbia University prove a thesis: that a person's upbringing and environment shaped a person's actions to a greater extent than genetic factors did. Together with another young scholar named Ruth Benedict, Mead set off to research the indigenous peoples of Samoa, spending nine months there—and the result of their time there was her 1928 book *Coming of Age in Samoa*.

The so-called revelations in this book left many in the academic world both thunder-struck and ecstatic. Margaret Mead described an idyllic island Eden in which people lived in an almost utopian harmony, with very little competition with one another and, most importantly, no draconian moral codes that restricted people's sexual behavior. Rather, teenage Samoans had many sexual partners and were encouraged to engage in this free love South Seas hook-up culture. As Margaret Mead wrote admiringly, a young Samoan girl "thrusts virtuosity away from her. … All of her interest is expended on clandestine sexual adventures."[3]

In other words, Christian morality and natural law were nothing but a hoax or a dangerous social construct.

The impact of Mead's book cannot be underestimated. According to one historian (writing in Ted Byfield's epic history of Christianity *The High Tide and the Turn**), "This would prove the most highly circulated anthropological book ever written. It became required reading for all first-year anthropology courses, and played a key role in shaping sex education, criminal law, government social policies, and the popular view of acceptable sexual conduct."[4]

In other words, it changed everything.

As John Horgan put it in the *Scientific American*, Mead's book "posed a challenge to Western sexual mores, which according to Mead inflicted needless suffering on young men and women. The metatheme of *Coming of Age* and all Mead's subsequent work was that the way things are is not the way they must or should be; we can choose to live in ways that make us happier and healthier. Her writings helped inspire feminism, the sexual revolution, the human potential movement and other countercultural trends during the 1960s."[5]

It is mind-boggling to realize when looking at the body of "scholarly work" produced by people such as Margaret Mead that brought about such cataclysmic changes in traditional

---

* Ted Byfield's twelve-volume series *The Christians: Their First Two Thousand Years* is the best overview of Christian history to surface in decades, providing an eminently readable and comprehensive narrative.

sexual mores that most of this work was shoddy research and wishful thinking. (For example, Margaret Mead's daughter later revealed that her thrice-married mother had many sexual relationships with women, including her fellow anthropologist Ruth Benedict. When she left for Samoa in 1926, Mead informed her husband that, "I'll not leave you unless I find someone I love more."[6]) Yet academic communities, eager for any shred of "evidence" that could disprove Christianity, seized onto Mead's work as yet more proof that Judeo-Christian values were outdated at best, and damaging at worst.

Much of Mead's work has since been revealed to be a hoax. Mead set off with conclusions she needed to prove, and simply found the information she needed to substantiate those conclusions, never living with one Samoan family or learning the language in her entire nine-month stay. Her information on the sexual culture of the Samoans, it turns out, came almost entirely from two young girls.

Mead, working on several projects at once, found herself running out of time to interview adolescent girls. So instead, she decided to befriend two of her female Samoan companions, win their trust, and then obtain from them the information on Samoan sexual culture that she needed. She did not realize that by asking the sensitive and explicit questions she was asking, she was breaching Samoan code of etiquette—and the girls responded by playfully feeding Mead precisely the type of information she wanted to hear. Mead was triumphant, feeling sure that her friendship with these girls had led her to discover the real truth about sexual customs in Samoa. The girls thought the joke they had played on the nosy Western anthropologist was quite funny. Little did they realize that their playful joke would end up informing entire fields of academic study in North America, with decidedly unfunny consequences.

When scholar Dr. Derek Freeman decided, years later, to follow up on Mead's research and travel to Samoa himself, he found that virtually all of her conclusions had been wrong.* Samoans

---

* Freeman's book *Margaret Mead in Samoa: The Making and Unmaking of an Anthropological Myth* lays out his findings in exhaustive detail.

held to a very strict, if not puritanical, code of sexual ethics. There was no South Seas hook-up culture. He even tracked down the two girls on whom Mead had based her analysis of Samoan sexual practices. As Byfield puts it: "He found these individuals, by now elderly women, and reminded them of Mead's visit. They began to giggle in embarrassment, he reported, recounting how they had told that white lady such awful lies and stories, not expecting her to believe them. They were sorry now to have so misled her, they said."[7]

Many in academia, seeing the foundation of so much of their worldview threatened, have savaged, personally maligned and slandered Freeman and other Mead critics. But most of them are now forced to admit that her work on the Samoans was fatally flawed. Unfortunately, our culture has already heeded the wishful thinking of Margaret Mead to such a great extent that much of the damage she has caused cannot be undone.

The Kinsey Reports

Mead was not the only one—another famous scientist, Dr. Alfred Kinsey, soon followed in her footsteps. His name will be immediately recognizable to most university graduates—he is heralded as the "Father of the Sexual Revolution." Originally a zoologist who specialized in studying wasps, Kinsey decided to branch out into a new field, that of "sexology." His resulting work, the *Kinsey Reports,* captured the imagination of the American people like nothing else had. His 1948 *Sexual Behavior in the Human Male* and his 1953 *Sexual Behavior in the Human Female* were cultural game-changers.

TIME magazine marveled at the reaction in its March 1, 1948 issue: "It weighed nearly three pounds, its 804 pages were a dreary morass of technical jargon and statistical charts, it cost $6.50. But last week the U.S. was taking to *Sexual Behavior in the Human Male*, commonly known as 'the Kinsey report' the way it had once taken to the Charleston, the yo-yo and the forcing two-bid. Not since *Gone with the Wind* had booksellers seen anything like it. Out less than two months, it had already sold 200,000 copies."[8]

It was the content, of course, that fascinated and perhaps titillated those who flocked out to purchase Kinsey's work. Everything that anyone had ever known about sex, it turned out, was wrong—because most of the country was engaging in sexual behavior that was at best immoral by traditional standards, and at worse deviant and downright shocking. Kinsey wasn't advising people to engage in these behaviors in his Kinsey Reports—at least not explicitly—he was saying that everyone was *already* engaging in them.

This too is taught in history classes as fact: My professor of American History taught our class during my first year in university that the Sexual Revolution hadn't actually happened—because Kinsey revealed that everyone had been scandalous hypocrites all along. No one had ever really believed in or bothered to adhere to Christian morality in regards to sexuality—and our society just needed Alfred Kinsey to come along and break the conspiracy of silence.

Just like Margaret Mead, however, Kinsey had more personal reasons for turning from the study of wasps to an exploration of sex. As one writer noted recently in a *New York Times* review, "Kinsey presented himself to the world as a scientist and a conventional husband and father—Professor Kinsey, whom even his wife called Prok.* It was an essential disguise for a man exploring controversial territory, but he was in fact far more complex. James H. Jones, a historian at the University of Houston, reveals in...[a] rich, awkward biography that Kinsey was energetically bisexual—Jones says 'homosexual' despite Kinsey's continuing sexual relationship with his wife —and a serious masochist. Kinsey also organized group sex among his senior staff, their spouses and outside volunteers, which he observed and had filmed, evidently to condition his investigators to their work and bond them together under his paternal authority as well as to record sexual behavior directly."[9]

And research they did. According to David Kupelian in *The Marketing of Evil*:

* An affectionate combination of "Professor" and "Kinsey."

> Funded by the prestigious Rockefeller Foundation and based on thousands of interviews, Kinsey had "discovered" that while American men of the World War II "greatest generation" pretended to be faithful and monogamous, virtually all of them—95 percent—were, according to 1948 law, sex offenders. Specifically, Kinsey claimed that 85 percent of males had intercourse prior to marriage, nearly 70 percent had sex with prostitutes, and 30-45 percent of husbands had extramarital affairs. Moreover, from 10 to 37 percent of men had engaged in homosexual acts, according to Kinsey. In fact, the oft-repeated claim that one in ten human beings is homosexual—a cornerstone of the "gay rights" movement until it was debunked—came directly from Kinsey's published research.[10]

In endless and graphic detail, Kinsey painted a picture of Americans as being amoral sexual animals in search of constant gratification.

When researching the true history of the Sexual Revolution and the cataclysmic cultural changes that swept the West over the past fifty years, it is constantly inferred that Christians have an inherent bias, making up a consistently noticeable double standard. That bias, of course, is their Christianity, which provides the lens through which they see the world and the foundation that underlies their work. Today more than ever, any opposition to abortion, pornography, or hook-up culture is often dismissed outright by intellectuals, the media, and the political establishment as Christian theology rather than evidence-based fact. The idea that those two concepts could coincide is ridiculed, although never disproven.

However, those intellectuals whose work supposedly debunked essential tenets of Christianity, especially in the area of sexuality, are bestowed with secular sainthood. Their biographies often read more like hagiographies, and even as their followers openly admit that cultural figures such as Margaret Mead and Alfred Kinsey were themselves flagrantly adulterous and promiscuous bisexuals, this obvious bias is never highlighted as evidence that they may have had powerful personal interests underlying the conclusions they brought forward.

A further and far more horrifying bias is evident in the historical treatment of Dr. Alfred Kinsey: The media, the scientific community, and the authorities ignored the fact that Kinsey facilitated the brutal sexual abuse of many children in his quest to prove that all human beings are sexual from birth until death. This information was not highlighted publicly until scholar Dr. Judith Reisman decided to take a look at Kinsey's research on child sexuality, which forms the foundation of modern sex education.

Her resulting book, *Kinsey, Sex and Fraud* is so devastating that it requires, as she asks of the reader in the book, the suspension of disbelief. Alfred Kinsey not only invented and falsified much of his data—he facilitated brutal sex crimes against children:

> Kinsey solicited and encouraged pedophiles, at home and abroad, to sexually violate from 317 to 2,035 infants and children for his alleged data on normal "child sexuality." Many of the crimes against children (oral and anal sodomy, genital intercourse and manual abuse) committed for Kinsey's research are quantified in his own graphs and charts. For example, "Table 34" on page 180 of Kinsey's "Sexual Behavior in the Human Male" claims to be a "scientific" record of "multiple orgasm in pre-adolescent males." Here, infants as young as five months were timed with a stopwatch for "orgasm" by Kinsey's "technically trained" aides, with one four-year old tested 24 consecutive hours for an alleged 26 "orgasms." Sex educators, pedophiles and their advocates commonly quote these child "data" to prove children's need for homosexual, heterosexual, and bisexual satisfaction via "safe-sex" education. These data are also regularly used to "prove" children are sexual from birth.[11]

The simple, chilling fact is that Alfred Kinsey and his companions actually defined children screaming, thrashing about in pain, passing out, and convulsing as "orgasm." Most of these children were too young to speak, so the only way they could express themselves was by showing just how much they were suffering. And, stop-watches in hand, the Kinsey men recorded their reactions as evidence of child sexuality. The evidence of those sex crimes would then be used to justify many things we now take for granted, like modern sex education.

It is not an accident that in all likelihood, you've never heard of the truth behind the Kinsey Reports. Just as with Dr. Derek Freeman and his exposé of Margaret Mead, the intellectual heirs of the Sexual Revolution have come out defending Dr. Alfred Kinsey fiercely by attempting to discredit and defame Dr. Judith Reisman in whichever way they can. Beginning in 1983 when Kinsey co-author Dr. Wardell Pomeroy refused to debate Reisman's findings on CNN and instead threatened to sue her, CNN's *Crossfire,* columnist Patrick Buchanan, Phil Donahue, and many other media outlets were threatened by the Kinsey Institute with lawsuits should they interview Dr. Reisman or feature her work.

Ten years later, Reisman discovered that the Kinsey Institute (which defines itself on its website as working "towards advancing sexual health and knowledge worldwide" and that "for over 60 years, the institute has been a trusted source for investigating and informing the world about critical issues in sex, gender and reproduction") had been distributing defamatory materials about her, informing people that her research was not peer-reviewed (it was) and asking universities to forbid her research. Included in these materials was a warning to the recipients that the information should "not be attributed to the Kinsey Institute."

The Kinsey Institute has had to fight Dr. Judith Reisman's revelations tooth and nail—because time and time again, she's illustrated that virtually everything about the Kinsey Reports is inaccurate and unreliable. Some time ago, I spoke with her about her book in which she systematically takes apart what she refers to as "Kinsey's defaming of the Greatest Generation":

> 1. [Dr. Kinsey's team] 'forced' subjects to give the desired answers to their sex questions, 2. Secretly trashed three

> quarters of their research data, and 3. Based their claims about normal males on a roughly 86 percent aberrant male population including 200 sexual psychopaths, 1,400 sex offenders and hundreds each of prisoners, male prostitutes and promiscuous homosexuals. Moreover, so few normal women would talk to them that the Kinsey team labeled women who lived over a year with a man 'married,' reclassifying data on prostitutes and other unconventional women as "Susie Homemaker."[12]

Dr. Reisman, unfortunately, is often a lone voice crying in the wilderness. The cultural elites are determined to hide the fact that the intellectuals that provided the framework for the Sexual Revolution were frauds. Instead, Kinsey is celebrated in Hollywood bio-pics and held up as one of our society's most influential thinkers. Unfortunately, he is.

The liberation of sex from love

It is impossible to underestimate the scale, speed and impact of the Sexual Revolution, set loose by the carefully orchestrated campaign Kinsey and his cohorts embarked on. There are many theories as to why a generation across the West—the United States, Canada, the United Kingdom, and beyond—decided to abandon the Judeo-Christian codes of sexual morality that had been the standard, to one extent or another, for well over a thousand years. It may have been the fact that a generation who had survived the Great Depression and fought World War II tried too hard to ensure that their children had everything, and literally spoiled them. It may have been the fact that official religion had not fared well through two world wars and its association with nationalism, and that Christianity was less and less a part of people's personal lives. It could be that the Vietnam War, with the US government drafting young men who wanted no part in it and sending them off to fight in the jungles a world away, was the final straw in an already stirring rebellion against authority that galvanized the Left across the Anglosphere. In all probability, it was a combination of all of these and more. But whatever it was, it changed everything for everyone.

A young man named Hugh Hefner led the charge, launching *Playboy* in December 1953, the first step in mainstreaming pornography. He had been inspired by the work of Alfred Kinsey, writing later that, "If Kinsey had done the research, I was the pamphleteer, spreading the news of sexual liberation through a monthly magazine."[13] Hefner married in 1949, but the marriage did not last long as he began to live out the "liberation" he championed. He separated from his wife in 1956—according to biographer Steven Watts, their marriage had been marked by Hefner's hedonism: "wife-swapping (Hefner slept with his sister-in-law), bisexuality, orgies, homemade porn films and serial affairs that go unmentioned here. Hefner had a bedroom next to his office and had taken to wearing his pyjamas to meetings as the boundaries between work and pleasure broke down." His divorce was finalized in 1959, and Hefner soon publicly advertised himself as the playboy embodied by his magazine.[14]

In short order, *Playboy* faced even cruder competitors as *Penthouse* and *Hustler* emerged, abandoning the veneer of sophistication Hefner tried to maintain for *Playboy* and selling precisely what the customers were looking for: raw, crude, and unattached sex. After all, everyone knew that no one bought *Playboy* for the articles—that was a joke that everyone was in on.

With the lid of Pandora's Box irreparably twisted from its hinges, pornography began to seep in everywhere—and women disinterested in visual porn began to drive a market for new obscenities. Novels like 1972's *The Flame and the Flower* and 1974's *Sweet Savage Love*, sex-drenched novels with graphic rape descriptions, sold millions of copies, the precursors to the soon-to-be booming Harlequin "romance" industry and the *50 Shades of Grey* craze. It's hard to discern whether or not these books were so popular because of changing attitudes on sexuality, or if these novels were part of the cultural engine changing those attitudes in the first place. Whatever the case, polls soon highlighted the fact that while Kinsey may have had to lie in the early 50's about American attitudes towards sex, Kinsey's prophetic deceits were becoming a reality of American life.

With the invention and dissemination of the birth control pill aiding the process, sexual promiscuity exploded into North American life. In his brilliant history *How We Got Here,* subtitled *The 70's: The Decade That Brought You Modern Life—For Better or Worse,* author David Frum lays out just how swiftly views on sex were transformed:

> As late as 1972, when the National Opinion Research Center first began probing male and female sexual attitudes, a solid majority of American women condemned premarital sex as immoral...only 20% said that premarital sex was 'not wrong at all'; almost twice as many men, 35 percent, did so...
>
> Between 1970 and 1980, those lingering inhibitions flew straight out the window. Feminists like Germaine Greer championed promiscuity as a means to break women's 'doglike' devotion to men, and the young women of the 1970s listened and obeyed. More than two-thirds of the women who turned eighteen between the end of the Korean War and the Kennedy inauguration acknowledged sleeping with only one man as of their thirtieth birthday—their fiancée or husband, presumably...
>
> Between 1972 and 1982, the proportion of American women who fully or conditionally endorsed premarital sex jumped by nearly 20 percentage points, to 58 percent, with fully 36 percent of women now espousing the ultra-permissive view that premarital sex was 'not wrong at all.' Tentatively at first, but with rising confidence, women were claiming unrestricted erotic freedom. Their parents sighed and shrugged their shoulders. In 1967, 85 percent of the parents of college-age young people condemned premarital sex as morally wrong; by 1979, only 37 percent of parents still held out against the trend of the times.[15]

Those numbers have not improved, and in our society today, the very idea that sex would be confined to a monogamous, heterosexual marriage is considered quaint and outdated, if not dangerous and "repressive." Overt sexuality is virtually everywhere—as with all revolutions, the carpet-baggers and the profiteers were the first to show up. As corporations realized that "free love" was on the "free market," they began to utilize sex as the most powerful tool in their arsenal. What pornographers and porn novelists could do, they could do, too. *Newsweek* magazine commented on the trend in 1967, as businesses, corporations and marketing firms began to get bolder:

> The old taboos are dead or dying. A new, more permissive society is taking shape. Its outlines are etched most prominently in the arts—in the increasing nudity and frankness of today's films, in the blunt, often obscene language seemingly endemic in American novels and plays, in the candid lyrics of pop songs and the undress of the avant-garde ballet, in erotic art and television talk shows, in freer fashions and franker advertising. And, behind this expanding permissiveness in the arts stands a society in transition, a society that has lost its consensus on such crucial issues as premarital sex…marriage, birth control and sex education; a society that cannot agree on standards of conduct, language, manners, on what can be seen and heard.[16]

It is hard to fully comprehend just how far our society has come since then, but one example may help to highlight it: In the early 1900s, people would be arrested for indecent exposure should they decide to expose too much skin on the beach—or anywhere else. It was generally accepted that civilized people covered up, and that immodesty was not a virtue. In fact, when designer Louis Reard announced in 1946 the release of his new bathing suit design—the bikini—not a single fashion model would agree to wear it for him. Instead, he had to hire a stripper to model it for a rather shocked and scandalized public.[17] Today most Christian families—even those who would consider themselves conservative—have been so brainwashed by the non-stop hyper-sexualization of everything around us that they don't even consider the bikini shocking or unacceptable. Most Christians don't think twice about teenagers heading off to hang out together wearing virtually nothing. That the Christians of a short 60 years ago would be busily arresting most of the Christians of today for public indecency is a powerful testimony to how far the Sexual Revolution has advanced.

Since the 1960s, this is the cultural water in which we've all been swimming. Hollywood, the music industry, television—each of these push the envelope with increasingly explicit sexuality of all forms. As each boundary comes down, the "artists" of our day plunge forward to the next one—and very rapidly, we all become used to it. Who can say anymore that they are shocked by sexually graphic billboards or advertisements? Who doesn't take it for granted that virtually every corporation and industry is going to use sex, innuendo, and scantily-clad models to sell virtually everything? It's very hard to be shocked or appalled by anything when you're bombarded by it, day in and day out. Instead, we become acclimatized to the culture and simply accept the new normal. What poet David Muar wrote of pornography certainly applies to our culture generally as well:

> Attributing pornography's growth to demand by individuals ignores what we know by experience: if one walks down the street and sees ten images of women as sexual objects, one may certainly be able to reject those images; yet it is also true that one will have to expend a greater amount of energy rejecting those images than if one saw only five or two or none at all. Assuming that human beings have only a limited amount of energy, it is obvious that the more images there are, the harder it will be for the individual to resist them; one must, after all, expend energy on other activities too...The greater the frequency of such images, the greater likelihood that they will overwhelm people's resistance. This fact is known, of course, by all those involved in advertising and media, and is readily accepted by most consumers—except when it comes to pornography.[18]

That, of course, is precisely how the sexualization of our culture has worn so many people down. When the academic and author Allan Bloom was trying to explain the marriage of the Sexual

Revolution and the corporations in his 1987 masterpiece *The Closing of the American Mind,* he painted a picture of the modern teenager that resonates still:

> Picture a thirteen-year-old boy sitting in the living room of his family home doing his math assignment while wearing his Walkman headphones or watching MTV. He enjoys the liberties hard won over centuries by the alliance of philosophic genius and political heroism, consecrated by the blood of martyrs; he is provided with comfort and leisure by the most productive economy ever known to mankind; science has penetrated the secrets of nature in order to provide him with the marvelous, lifelike electronic sound and image reproduction he is enjoying. And in what does progress culminate? A pubescent child whose body throbs with orgasmic rhythms; whose feelings are made articulate in hymns to the joys of onanism or the killing of parents; whose ambition is to win fame and wealth in imitating the drag-queen who makes the music. In short, life is made into a nonstop, commercially prepackaged masturbational fantasy.[19]

From the bedroom to the street

"There's no place for the state in the bedrooms of the nation," a tousled, sweaty-looking Pierre Trudeau told a clump of reporters outside the Canadian House of Commons in 1967. It was, history now tells us, an iconic moment. Trudeau's phrase rapidly became a slogan: "The state has no business in the bedrooms of the nation"—which, in turn, was becoming a secular dogma.

Across North America and the morally ravaged husk of what was once known as "Christendom," the sexual fascists demanded that we all recognize that the only Truth was that there was no Truth, the only absolute was moral relativism, and that the churches slam their doors and keep their meddlesome standards of morality to themselves. They were seemingly oblivious to the fact that they were imposing a new morality of their own—one without a foundation, without objectivity, and completely based on feelings. It was philosophical iconoclasm, if not vandalism; as future Canadian Prime Minister Pierre Trudeau noted wryly in the same interview, the libertine legislation he was proposing (the 1969 Omnibus Bill that decriminalized abortion, homosexuality, and liberalized divorce) "knocked down a lot of totems and [would override] a lot of taboos."

Traditionally speaking—from the Victorian era (inaccurately famous for flaunting prudishness) to shortly after the Second World War—Western civilization was generally of the opinion that being civilized meant acting civilized, and that one of the prime indicators of that was the lack of public disrobing as well as a consensus that love-making should remain an intimate experience behind closed doors. Then the Sexual Revolution arrived, with all that it entailed—the gay liberation movement, the radical feminist movement, and the indiscriminate propagation of "free love." All of these considered public nudity as a means of making a point, however mysteriously.* While Trudeau and countless other less eloquent culture warriors "courageously" spoke up for their right to live life without irritating inhibition and claimed to be removing the State from the bedroom, what they actually did was *open the bedroom door and invite it onto the streets.*

We've gone from one extreme to the other. On the one side of the spectrum there is mistaken prudishness: the damaging idea that sex is somehow shameful. On the other side, we have objectively crude and wildly exhibitionist Gay Pride Parades and so-called Slut Walks. These are not considered to be optional festivals hosted by tiny minority groups. No, politicians who refuse to attend events like the Gay Pride Parade are loudly called out as heretics by the high priests of the New Moral Order, which is of course not an order at all, but a proud lack thereof. They don't want the State to be outside the bedroom anymore, they want the State in the bedroom—loudly applauding the acts they see taking place, refraining from any judgement but one of approval, and perhaps even paying for pills and bits of latex to ensure that such acts do not go awry and result in reproduction or infection.

* A feminist baring her chest to protest misogynist men defining her worth by it has always struck me as somewhat counter-productive.

We're now ordered to close the church door, but open the bedroom door. Morals and values have no place in public, while at the same time the Sexual Revolutionaries demand that we fund their practices with our tax dollars, and that churches accept (if not endorse) their practices without moral condemnation. It would seem that there is such a thing as bad churches, but no such thing as bad sex. "Good sex," of course, means simply that at least one of the humans engaging in the interaction experienced some measure of fleeting enjoyment. A highly subjective and meaningless way of describing something—as G.K. Chesterton once noted, "The word 'good' has many meanings. For example, if a man were to shoot his grandmother at a range of five hundred yards, I should call him a good shot, but not necessarily a good man."

Public nudity is accepted in many places, but any reference to God and the Moral Law are definitely not, as governing bodies consistently confuse freedom *of* religion with freedom *from* religion. Prayers are not welcome in public, but privates are. The Emperor has no clothes, and is quite enjoying it—so long as the chilly breezes of moral truth don't leak out of drafty cathedrals to cause shriveling discomfort.

It is shocking to consider just how far today's society has fallen from what is considered suitable for public consumption and what is not. It borders on the absurd—a public Christian prayer might offend a non-Christian, but a simulated orgy disguising itself as a parade surely will not offend anyone. Many cities fund the Gay Pride Parade, which regularly features nudity among other bizarre displays of sexuality.

This new morality, to paraphrase David Frum, believes it more honorable to fornicate in the mud of Woodstock than to fight in the mud of Guadalcanal. This new morality, as the coming chapters will illustrate, is one with dangerous consequences. As is proven by the shattered corpses of aborted pre-born children brought about by millions of frivolous coital encounters, the Sexual Revolutionaries may not have found something they're willing to die for. But they have found something they're willing to kill for.

Our Brave New World: Sexual "rights" replace all of our other rights

When abortion activists came shrieking with rage at Canadian Member of Parliament Stephen Woodworth's suggestion that a committee examine human life in the womb in 2013, he was somewhat surprised. When the Canadian government kowtowed to feminist hysteria and shut down his colleague Mark Warawa's motion to condemn gender-selection abortion, Woodworth noticed a trend—and coined a new term. What we're seeing is "abortionism," he told me in an interview. "Abortionism" is essentially a philosophy that raises abortion to a sacred status, above all other democratic principles. I agree with Mr. Woodworth, but I think the problem goes much deeper than abortion. Abortion's now-sacred status is symptomatic of something far more sinister: the sweeping success of the Sexual Revolution. So-called "sexual rights" are now considered to be the most important "rights" our society has, and take precedence over all other rights, regardless of how fundamental they are.

Freedom of speech? This is now a concept that does not apply, for example, to any sort of pro-life activism, especially and ironically on university campuses, once lauded as the marketplaces of ideas. Pornography, nude demonstrations, and virtually any form of sex-related activism is welcome—unless you happen to be *opposing* something, in which case it is not. When I was in university, for example, our "Cemetery of the Innocents" display was trampled and destroyed by a student politician who then took to the campus paper to refer to us as "the Hitler Youth." On campus after campus across North America, feminists respond to pro-life activism the same way: Shut down the debate. Almost every pro-life activist I know has been censored on his or her university campus in some way or another—and usually with the endorsement, if not assistance, of the university administration.

The same applies to the right to educate your children as you see fit. Increasingly, adherents of the Sexual Revolution are realizing that in order to get the upcoming generation of Christians to accept the New Sexual Order, they will have to force it on them.

Specifically, mandate new "sex education." Christian schools and home-schoolers frustrate them, because they can no longer teach children about masturbation and anal sex in fifth grade. As Wendy Shalit highlights in her magnificent book *A Return to Modesty*, much of the public education system is now the systematic destruction of innocence. And if the powers that be have their way, soon you won't be able to opt out.

Religious liberty is being dispensed with at an alarming rate as well. After all, our culture has abandoned religious values. Once we've chiseled and hacked the last of the Ten Commandments monuments from in front of the last courthouses, we can put those beliefs in the trash can alongside it. Businesses that disagree with gay marriage are being forced to shut down. Churches in Denmark have already been ordered to perform gay weddings, and there's no reason to think that such things won't soon begin to happen here in North America. Our tax dollars are used to fund Pride Parades that resemble public orgies. The Sexual Revolutionaries are not, for the most part, about living and let live. They are about compulsory acceptance.

All rights are now subject to sexual rights.

How We Got Here

The Sexual Revolutionaries didn't just change history. They rewrote it, because that's what revolutionaries always do. This struck me vividly when I was traveling in China, and our tour guide, a pretty young woman named Anna, was taking my friend and I from the Forbidden Palace to Tiananmen Square to Mao Tse-Tung's Mausoleum, where the dead dictator still lies in state in a glass-covered coffin. After listening to Anna praise Mao for hours, I asked her how she could possibly believe he was good for China when, by some estimates, he presided over the deaths of nearly seventy million people.

First she was irritated, and then agitated. After informing me that Mao was a great leader, she ended our discussion by announcing, "Denying Mao would be like denying Communist Party!" And with that, historical truth was placed firmly in the backseat to ideological obligation.

In order to understand the sex-driven lunacy and carnage that has gripped our culture on virtually every front, we have to put history back in the front seat. We have to honestly analyze and understand how we reached this point, so that we can begin to realize what we can do—not to return, but to rebuild. To equip our children and the upcoming generation with the truth of what has actually taken place, and why it is that we believe what we do.

This is precisely what Ted Byfield told me when I asked him what young people could do to begin the process of cultural renewal. Read history, he told me urgently. People will be stunned to find out what actually happened—"they will be astonished at the things we've done in [the last] century that made no sense at all. What should be emphasized in your generation is to *find out what happened*. In other words, *read history*."

He's right. Once we know what has *happened*, we will have a better sense of what is *happening*, and have vital context for the spreading social decay we are witnessing. That decay, as we will see, has become our culture's new normal.

Chapter 2

Hook-up Culture and the New Normal

But sometime during sophomore year, she got tired of relationships fading away, 'no end, no beginning.' Guys would text her at eleven PM, 'wanna hang out?' but never during the day. Like many of the college-age women I talked to, Tali and her friends seemed much more sexually experienced and knowing than my friends at college. They were as blasé about blow jobs and anal sex as the one girl I remember from my freshman dorm whom we all judged as destined for tragic early marriage or a string of abortions. But they were also more innocent. When I asked Tali what she really wanted, she said, 'Some guy to ask me out on a date to the frozen yogurt place.'

—Hanna Rosin, *The End of Men and the Rise of Women*

The preceding quote, from journalist Hanna Rosin's 2013 book, is a profoundly depressing one. Innocence, once greatly prized and ardently protected, is now something virtually unknown in the culture at large. As I wrote in Chapter 1, it's not actually that Western youth are rejecting Christian teachings concerning sexuality as much as they are completely unaware of them. The idea that sex is a deeply private and intimate experience that should be limited to a man and a woman within marriage is one that is completely foreign to them. Condoms and birth control are distributed at high schools and universities everywhere, and so-called "sex education" is more about enabling and facilitating rather than advocating any sort of moral framework for intimacy. Parents, by and large, no longer even try to raise their children to view sex as something exclusively for within marriage. After all, the vast majority of them didn't wait either.

I interact with university and high school students all the time, and with the exception of some Christian high school students, I have never met anyone who had considered abstinence before marriage as an option. One angry young high school girl demanded to know why I, as a male, should have anything to say on the abortion issue. I asked her if she felt boys should respect her, and whether she thought a boy who was pressuring her to have sex should perhaps also be ready to commit to her, love her, and raise any children that might result from such activities. "*Yes*," she responded wistfully, after considering this for a few minutes. She'd never even considered the possibility that might be an option. I left that conversation feeling heartbroken for the millions of boys and girls who have never been presented with the idea that intimacy could be something so much more beautiful.

But after all, where would they have come into contact with the Christian ideal of sexuality? Hollywood relentlessly promotes the idea that love and sex are the same thing, that pleasure and happiness can be conflated. As I will illustrate in the next two chapters, many of them have their first exposure to sex by coming into contact with pornography, and assume falsely that this is "real" sex. Virginity is mocked throughout the entertainment industry as an inconvenience to be gotten rid of at the earliest opportunity. The music industry shrieks anthems of lust into the ears of children at younger and younger ages. And the result is nearly always the same. Broken culture, broken homes, broken hearts.

Promiscuity, even predatory promiscuity, has been so normalized and so mainstreamed that virtually every comedy sitcom on television can joke about girls who seem on board for casual coitus as having "daddy issues," a line that invariably causes raucous canned laughter. I often wonder if people know what they are laughing at. "Daddy issues" actually refers most often to girls who grew up without the presence of a father in the home to begin with, and thus crave the male attention they were denied. Boys and girls, we used to understand, need both a mother and a father, and the absence of one will invariably cause a lack of balance. Unfortunately, girls seeking love "in all the wrong places," as the song goes, will often fall prey to the types of carnivorous playboys that are portrayed as lovable sex hounds on television sitcoms. "She's needy, she's vulnerable—I'm thinking *cha-ching!*" said playboy Joey Tribiani on the smash-hit 90s sitcom *Friends*. In other words, she didn't have a father—but I can use that to psychologically manipulate her for sex! *Hilarious, right?*

Not really. I can't quite figure out how preying on the brokenness in one another can be considered funny.

The hook-up culture

For this hook-up culture to come into being, there had to be a profound change in sexual values to begin with. As I outlined in the previous chapter, that took place with the Sexual Revolution. Kathleen Bogle, an assistant Professor of Sociology and Criminal Justice at Philadelphia's LaSalle University examined these trends in detail in her book-length 2008 study *Hooking Up: Sex, Dating, and Relationships on Campus*.

In trying to explain how hook-up culture came to be, Bogle writes that "The 1960s are widely known as a time of great change throughout our society, particularly among the youth. The advent and increased availability of the birth control pill coupled with a liberalization of attitudes toward sexuality led to changes in what was socially acceptable to do sexually. In fact, intercourse became thought of as a sign of intimacy and physical pleasure rather than merely a means of reproduction. With these reproductive and attitudinal changes came changes in sexual behavior."[20]

In fact, in her analysis, Bogle notes that on campus, the "least likely to participate in hooking up are racial minorities [and] students who are *very* religious," emphasis hers. In other words, it takes powerful moral convictions to avoid joining in once you arrive on the sexual playground our universities have become.[21]

Of course, Christians never saw sex as "merely a means of reproduction," which is why intercourse was, once upon a time, referred to as "making love." Sex, in the Judeo-Christian context, was intended to be unitive and procreative, serving to both bond the man and wife to one another and from that bond create the miracle of new life. Instead, the hook-up culture serves up a crude and crass imitation of genuine intimacy, a scenario in which boys and girls, men and women can extract brief pleasure from one another before moving on to the next partner and repeating the scenario.

Not only has the unitive aspect of sex been forgotten, considering the fact that the sexual player has no intention of "uniting" with the other for anything beyond physical satisfaction—but the procreative aspect of sex has been forgotten, as well. The widespread availability of contraception has created what many Christian thinkers refer to as "the contraceptive mentality"—the idea that sex and procreation are only incidentally linked. Men seem to believe sex is only "recreational," having forgotten the biological reality that they possess reproductive organs, not recreational ones. Considering the omnipresence of pornography in the lives of most modern men, this shouldn't be particularly surprising.

Lest you should think this an exaggeration, I could easily cite dozens of examples of young men expressing confusion when sex results in pregnancy. For example, one fellow at the University of Calgary—he was in third year philosophy—approached me at a pro-life display and demanded to know what he was to do if he got a girl pregnant "by accident."

By accident? I wondered. *Did he trip and fall, or something?* If someone engages in sexual intercourse, they have no right to be surprised when it *works like it is supposed to* and the creation of new life occurs.

Another university student informed me that he had gotten his girlfriend pregnant by mistake. "I don't know how that happened!" he whined.

"Really?" I replied. "Are you *sure* you don't know how that happened? Because I wasn't even there and I can tell you how it happened."

He got the point, eventually. But these students are simply

manifestations of a generation of males who believe that they have the *right* to sex without "consequences." Nature must be suspended to permit their libidos free reign. While we know that for every action in nature, there is an equal and opposite reaction, our sex-driven culture ignores this when it comes to indulging their sexual whims.

Even medical professionals can suspend reality. A forty-two-year-old doctor in Toronto recently sued a woman he had been casually sleeping with for getting pregnant, claiming emotional damages. He, like a good post-modern gentleman, assumed the woman he was extracting fleeting pleasure from had turned her reproductive system into a chemical playground to ensure that they could continue to have casual coitus free of any consequences. When she got pregnant and refused to get an abortion, he was petulantly furious. As the *Toronto Star* reported:

> To use the language of the statement of claim, PP was emotionally harmed because he was deprived of the choice of falling in love, marrying, enjoying married life and, when he and his wife thought 'the time was right,' having a baby," the judge wrote in his 18-page ruling.[22]

You read that right. This adult doctor was upset that his promiscuity had resulted in pregnancy before he could attain his fairy tale ending, which presumably could have only come about if he had stopped sleeping with "some random girl" as he put it, and decided to enter a relationship with someone he actually intended to marry. But men in our culture believe so firmly in their right to sex without consequences that this presumably intelligent man actually had the audacity to lawyer up and take his grievance against nature to court.

What can you expect when this sexually-charged atmosphere is cultivated on the most prestigious campuses? Even Yale University, from which the eminent theologian Jonathan Edwards once graduated, is now home to scenes of exuberant depravity. Nathan Harden described the sexual circus in his brilliant 2012 book *Sex and God at Yale: Porn, Political Correctness, and a Good Education Gone Bad*. "No fewer than seventeen official events were held during Sex Week 2008," he wrote with distaste, "ranging from a porn-star look-alike contest (judged by a real-life porn film director), to safe-sex workshops, to lectures on the female orgasm. The event was so chock-full of goodies that organizers were forced to stretch Sex "Week" into eleven continuous days of nonstop sex, sexuality, sexiness, and sensationalism."[23]

Harden places the blame for the misogyny metastasizing in our culture firmly on feminism and the Sexual Revolution, noting that while their stated intention was to liberate women and liberate sexuality, all that seems to have happened is that men have been liberated from their trousers and the need to treat their sexual partners like actual human beings worthy of dignity. Something was lost, Harden writes, when we decided that intimacy could be a casual thing:

> When it comes to sex, a major source of a woman's power is the control she exercises over her own body. It is only if she gives this up and conforms to a typical college existence, consisting of endless hookups with men she barely knows, that a woman really loses power in relationships. At Yale, a guy doesn't have to ride thirty miles or stand on his head. He only has to show up at a random party and talk to some girl for a few minutes—and make sure she has a few drinks. It's so easy. This is why sexual liberation never really empowered women in the way it was supposed to. A woman is truly objectified when men don't even have to get to know her in order to get her into bed…I know it sounds very 1950s. But playing hard to get might not have been a bad idea for feminists, if power is what they were after.[24]

Hanna Rosin, a feminist writer, disagreed strongly with Harden in her own analysis of campus hookup culture. "To put it crudely… feminist progress is largely dependent on hook-up culture," she stated bluntly, "To a surprising degree, it is women—not men—who are perpetuating the culture, especially in school, cannily manipulating it to make space for their success, always keeping their own ends in mind. Today's college girl likens a serious suitor to an accidental pregnancy in the nineteenth century: a danger to be avoided at all costs."[25]

Keep in mind that Rosin is the same journalist who noted, in the quote that prefaced this chapter, the desire of female students not for more sexual adventure, but merely to be asked out on an actual date. To have a real conversation with someone interested in not just her body, but in her opinions, her intellect, and her life. Quite simply, these women want to be treated as people, not as an acceptable collection of body parts for the sexual use of a male stranger. Not all proverbs are accurate, but the cliché that men use love to get sex and women use sex to get love is a cliché for a reason: it's often true. And in today's hook-up culture, women are often faced with an unpleasant choice: Stay out of relationships, or engage in the hook-up culture and lose the respect of men.

Hanna Rosin may be right when she states that women now play the game, too, although she brushes over the sad fact that our hyper-sexualized culture now places expectations on women and girls that are far worse than anything we saw before the rise of feminism. But beyond that, even women engaging in the hook-up culture seem to realize that it degrades them in some fundamental way. Dr. Kathleen Bogle noted this with surprise in her study of hook-up culture:

> Some college students in my sample indicated that they would go further sexually with someone during a hookup if they did not really like the person or did not think that there was any chance for a relationship with that person. On the face of it, this seems illogical. Why would students be more sexual with someone they did not really like or did not envision as a potential partner? Many college students realized that getting too sexual with a hookup partner early on is not a good way to begin a relationship. Students indicated that you should 'take it slow' with someone you really liked and 'get to know each other' for a while. Too much sexual interaction in the early stages of meeting someone was seen as ruining any chance you might otherwise have to pursue a relationship with that person.[26]

Interesting, isn't it? Hookups are not only devoid of intimacy, they are often *specifically and intentionally so*. Bogle quotes students who admit that in spite of their enlightened post-Sexual Revolution mindsets, they still looked down on those who consistently slept around. Men admitted to losing respect for women who engaged in promiscuous behavior, and women admitted to delaying sexual contact with those they hoped to pursue a long-term relationship with to ensure that the men would respect them and maintain an interest in them. At the end of the day, it seems, we cannot escape our desire for true love and intimacy in an exclusive, monogamous relationship. Which is why, as GK Chesterton noted, "It may be conceded to the mathematicians that four is twice two. But two is not twice one; two is two thousand times one. That is why, in spite of a hundred disadvantages, the world will always return to monogamy."

Throughout Kathleen Bogle's study of campus hook-up culture, Nathan Harden's account of university sex culture, Hanna Rosin's analysis of shifting gender roles in the 21st century, and many other studies on today's sexual chaos, one thing shines through. Over and over again, we see that people aren't happy, and women least of all. Bogle states bluntly that men have all the power in today's new sexual dynamics, and that women are often left wishing for relationships that cannot be attained. Men no longer need to commit to a woman to get sex, and thus often choose to live in a state of pseudo-adolescence, skipping from one hook-up to the next. Rosin defends the hook-up culture as necessary to feminism, but the malaise and longing for something more shines through in her interviews with women too.

Even smutty films put out by Hollywood can't deny our culture's instinctive recognition that hook-up culture doesn't work, and that it certainly doesn't bring happiness. In every film where "friends with benefits" are featured and hook-up culture is celebrated, inevitably, the guy and the girl find themselves wanting more, and choose to enter into an exclusive relationship. But unfortunately for the Sexual Revolution's Lost Generation, Hollywood happy endings are hard to come by in the real world.

Sexual re-education

Not only are happy endings hard to come by, our society has spent the last few decades actively stacking the deck against them. The public school system now actively promotes both extra-marital sex and "alternative" sexual lifestyles as normal and healthy, completely ignoring the fact that most young people do, in fact, want to get married one day.

During a heated public debate surrounding sex education in Ontario, Canada, *National Post* journalist Peter Jon Mitchel complained about this fact, noting that today's sex education is both counter-productive and inadequate:

> About 88 per cent of Canadian teens say they expect to marry someday. This is a good thing: there is ample evidence that marriage remains the gold standard for family formation, offering benefits to adults and children alike.
>
> That said, marriage rates have been in general decline over the last number of decades. And Canadians who do marry are waiting longer, entering marriage for the first time at an average age of about 30. This means people entering marriage have often accumulated more than a decade of dating.
>
> So just how does any young person find their way to life-long marriage? There are many answers to that. One place they are extraordinarily unlikely to get any assistance is at school in sex education.
>
> Others have already noted the absence of love in current sex education curricula. Importantly, a discussion of marriage is likewise absent.
>
> This should give us pause, since research shows that teen relationship history is linked to future romantic patterns. Teens who engage in numerous short-term relationships or non-romantic sexual relationships are less likely to enter stable relationships as young adults.[27]

But unfortunately, today's sex re-education is about imparting a certain worldview to the students under the guise of a false neutrality. Boundaries are still discussed, yes—but those boundaries are not moral ones. Those boundaries are instead the flimsy barriers of "consent" and "comfort level," along with sporadic warnings about the legality of various sex acts and, if the students are fortunate, some muted warnings about the growing prevalence of sexually transmitted diseases. Of course, the "neutrality" is a farce—by replacing the moral boundaries of the Judeo-Christian tradition with the Sexual Revolution's so-called boundary of "do what feels right for you," a powerful and toxic message is being imparted to students: Sex has no purpose other than to please you. It can be precisely what you want it to be.

This is precisely why so many Christian parents are fundamentally opposed to the idea that the education system or the State has any business imparting "education" of sexual matters to their children. That is, they say, not the task of the education system. And when the government disagrees and implements sex education anyways, parents are justifiably suspicious that another agenda is at play—that it is not simply the mechanics of sex that the state wants to teach, but rather the idea that all sexual activity is morally permissible and that these ideas should be ingrained into children at a very young age to ensure that they stick.

Peter Hitchens, a well-known journalist, author, and cultural commentator from Great Britain, has had much to say about the idea of modern sex education in his various writings and media interviews.* For more insight into how modern sex education in the West came about, I decided to interview him. According to his analysis, the suspicions of many parents are absolutely correct. In his view, the entire concept of sex education fails on its own terms.

"The problem with sex education," he told me by phone, "is that the ostensible purpose for which it is advocated turns out not to be true. I did a study a few years ago of the development of sex education in my own country, and what I found is that it's been justified really since the middle part of the Second World War, when of course there were a lot of venereal diseases, on

---

* His books *The Rage Against God* and *The Abolition of Britain*, among others, are brilliant and worthwhile reads.

the basis that if people were better educated about it, then it would reduce the amount of sexually transmitted disease and the amount of unwanted pregnancy. And yet if you watch the figures for both sexually transmitted disease and for unwanted pregnancy, and increasingly now for abortion, we find that despite the greater and greater extent of sex education in our society, more and more frankness about sex, and more and more pornography (which is also supposed to end repression), the number of people becoming pregnant when they didn't want to continues to rise and the number of people contracting sexually transmitted diseases continues to rise."

This is partially because, as *National Post* columnist George Jonas wrote during one sex education controversy, educating young people in an activity will of course increase that activity. Thus, the risk of abortion, sexually transmitted disease, and teenage pregnancy will only go up. If sex education's intent, however, is not simply to prevent these things, but rather to re-educate, then it still can suit the purposes of the State quite nicely.

"It is said," Hitchens noted, "that Gyorgy Lukas, who was commissar for education in the short-lived Bela Kun Soviet Government in Hungary in 1918, openly said that the purpose of sex education when he introduced it then—I think he was probably the first person to do so—was to debauch the minds and morals of religiously-brought up young women particularly. It seems to me to make a certain amount of sense...because the kinds of things that people are taught in sex education are disinhibiting things. When I was in school no one ever mentioned masturbation. It would have been extremely bad manners to mention it anywhere, let alone for an adult teacher to talk to quite young children about it and about other sexual practices in class. The moment these things start being discussed, it disinhibits people, it takes restraints off them that previously were there. Now you may believe, and a lot of people do believe and have believed for many years, that these inhibitions are bad for us. That's a point of view, I don't happen to share it, and if you follow that belief as a parent, I suppose you're entitled to introduce your child to this sort of thing as early an age as you wish in a free country, but what bothers us in many cases [is that] parents don't realize what is being done in classrooms until after it's happened."

"Discussing these things in the way that they're discussed [makes these] things sound normal," Hitchens pointed out. "So it's assumed that children will have underage sex or unmarried sex or promiscuous sex, and it's assumed that they will do so, and all the precautions they're supposed to take is based on this idea that this will happen. 'If you can't be good, be careful.'"

That, of course, is why our public schools are so involved in handing out condoms and ensuring ready access to birth control pills—because they assume that people, even children, are entirely incapable of abstaining from sex outside of marriage. Sex education, in essence, proceeds directly out of that assumption. And that assumption is very much promoted by our current political class.

"There [are] politics in sex," says Peter Hitchens. "Much of those politics are about the family and the State. The state is increasingly hostile to the strong family, and the strong family is sustained by lifelong marriage and by a pretty stern and puritan attitude towards sexual relations—whereas the strong state benefits in many ways, as does modern commerce and the modern employer, from weak marriages and relaxed sexual relations. There's also the point that Aldous Huxley makes, which is that we are increasingly going to embrace our own enslavement in the pursuit of pleasure, which [is a point] I believe actually the Marxist historian Eric Hobsbawm made... that there is absolutely no congruence in human history between sexual freedom and political freedom. Slaves have always been allowed to copulate, what they haven't been allowed to do is marry."

"And this," Hitchens continued, "is an extremely important point. There is no necessary connection between a society which is sexually free and sexually uninhibited, and a society that is politically free and has free speech and freedom of assembly. It doesn't necessarily follow at all. So [this is] a very, very profound philosophical battle about the nature of society, and it needs to be conducted in a very serious fashion. The difficulty is in finding anyone to give you a hearing."

It's a fascinating perspective, especially coming from someone who was once a radical Trotskyist as Hitchens was. When I pointed this out to him, Hitchens responded by noting that this is precisely the reason he is so well-versed in the way the Left thinks and does business.

"I decided to stop believing it because it seemed to me to be morally wrong and highly dangerous," Hitchens told me. "But the great advantage which it gives me is that I know what left-wing people say and think in private when they're not trying to please people on television shows. I know just how dogged and devastating this project is, which they want, and I know that the fundamental engine of left-wing activity, really since the 1960s, has not been to seize the post office and the barracks and the railway station; it's been to seize the television station and the newspaper and the university, and to obtain victory through capturing the minds of people, and also to alter society not through the nationalizing of railways, but through the nationalizing of childhood."

The nationalizing of childhood. A chilling idea, but one that makes much sense. Give to the State and its education system the task of teaching children what to believe and which values to hold, and you've essentially co-opted the family structure.

"When they say children should speak for themselves," Hitchens pointed out, "what they actually mean is that the parents should be removed from the discussion. They don't actually want them to speak for themselves; they want the children to do what *they* want them to do, and they know the parental home is the biggest obstacle to this thing."

This is why many states seek to ban practices that threaten this goal, like homeschooling: "There's a certain amount of it in Britain, it's actually illegal in Germany to this day because of the National Socialist law passed under Hitler, which has never been repealed, and attempts are being made to restrict it in Britain. They're in their infancy, but they're on their way, and

I think parental resistance to it on that scale is probably the only effective answer. You say, 'Alright, well if you feel that this is how you want to drive your power into my home and into my life, then I thank you very much, but I'm not going to let you. We'll educate our children at home.' And quite honestly, I don't know what your public school system is like, but if it's anything remotely like ours, it'll probably come up with a much better general education on top."

Parental resistance is, at the end of the day, the answer to the State's attempt to educate and re-educate children, and that is already increasingly difficult. In many places in Canada and the United States, governments are stepping in and demanding that acceptance of certain sexual behaviors be taught. Officials are objecting to parents who want to opt their children out of sex education. And increasingly, Christian schools are being told that the day is soon coming when they will no longer be allowed to teach sexuality from the Christian point of view. Many people, after all, consider that point of view to be hateful and harmful.

First and foremost, it is essential that parents take the responsibility of educating their children on sexuality seriously. This is something that Christians have often done quite badly, but it is the most effective way of inoculating the youth against many of the damaging ideas promoted everywhere in our society. If we teach our children nothing about biblical sexuality and send them out into a hedonistic and exhibitionist culture, we are practically guaranteeing that they will not be able to withstand the poisonous intellectual onslaught and torrent of temptation.

I was fortunate enough to have a father who sat me down when he realized that I was beginning to grow curious about such things. He explained, in a remarkably calm and not at all awkward fashion, what sexuality was all about. He then asked me if I had any questions, and answered all of my disjointed and hilariously incoherent questions with great aplomb, knowing that it was important that I felt taken seriously. If he had laughed at any of my questions, or even hinted at amusement, I would have immediately become uncomfortable and turned elsewhere for answers. Friends on the playground at school, for example, or perhaps the Internet. Instead, my first exposure to the idea of sexuality was a Christian one—and because Dad had the good sense to position himself as the source of my information, I consistently came back to him with all of my questions. He ensured that he, as my parent, was the one informing my view of sexuality, and that is precisely why when those ideas were challenged as I progressed through high school and into university, I discovered I had a foundation to stand on when I felt unsure. I could write an entirely separate book on the many reasons I feel grateful to my parents, but that gift was certainly one of the greatest.

The swamps of sexuality

Sow the wind, reap the whirlwind. Sex education has been tremendously successful—and a brief look at the culture tells a rather sickening story.

While the entertainment industry, the media, and institutions of learning pretend that the Sexual Revolution has made people more likely to be happy and free, in reality, it has only really made people more likely to have herpes. Society's cesspools of promiscuity and hook-up culture have proven a breeding ground teeming with disease and infection. Prior to 1960, the only two sexually transmitted diseases that occurred with much frequency were gonorrhea and syphilis. Today, there are more than 25 categories of sexually transmitted diseases for participants of the hook-up culture to worry about—not 25 diseases, mind you—25 *categories*.

You're not likely to hear the term "sexually transmitted disease" in sex education classes anymore. The term disease was swapped out for "infection" in recent years in order to reduce the stigma of having contracted one. An "infection," of course, sounds far more treatable than a "disease." Never mind that more than 20,000 American women will become infertile as the result of STDs every year.[28] Never mind that the Canadian Cancer Society has been warning incessantly that human papillomavirus (HPV), can lead to many types of cancer, including cervical cancer. Never mind that many across North America have received the terrifying news that they are HIV positive—or that many have lost loved ones to the resulting lethal disease of AIDS. We must all pretend that the Emperor is wearing clothes, even though he is not, and even though we can see that he has genital warts.

The STD epidemic makes headlines occasionally, but not often—and certainly not in proportion to the prevalence of these diseases or the impact on average North Americans. When the Public Health Agency of Canada released a report on "the State of Public Health in Canada" in 2013, they called STDs "the never-ending threat." The Chief Public Health Officer then began the report by listing off a series of trends that you certainly won't find taught in high schools:

- Sexually transmitted infections are a significant and increasing public health concern in Canada and worldwide.
- In Canada, reported rates of chlamydia, gonorrhea and syphilis have been steadily rising since the late 1990s.
- Young Canadians have the highest reported rates of sexually transmitted infections; however, increasing numbers of cases are being reported among middle-aged and older adults.
- Untreated sexually transmitted infections can have long-term health outcomes.
- Preventing and reducing the spread and impact of infection involves individual and broader commitments.[29]

Nearly every sexually transmitted disease is on the rise in Canada. Chlamydia rates have increased every single year since 1997, with a 72% increase between 2001 and 2010. Gonorrhea rates increased 53.4% between 2001 and 2010, and have not stopped rising—with rates among females between the age of 15 and 19 years of age being four times the national average. Syphilis rates have skyrocketed, rising 456.7% between 2001 and 2010, with especially dramatic increases among "men who have sex with men." Additionally, the Public Health Agency of Canada "estimates that 71,200 Canadians were living with HIV infection (including AIDS) in 2011, an 11.4% increase from the 2008 estimate of 64,000."[30]

The situation in the United States is even worse. For example, AIDS first surfaced in 1981, and the Center for Disease Control estimates that over 1.8 million people have been infected with HIV since then. That includes the more than 650,000 people who have died from AIDS already, with the homosexual community being particularly ravaged. While HIV rates are levelling off for women, they are still on the rise in men who have sex with men. These facts, published officially by the federal government, never gain much attention.[31] The cause of gay liberation is not served by reminding people of the diseases that so often accompany homosexual activity.

And that is only the tip of the iceberg. There are *over 20 million* new cases of sexually transmitted diseases in the United States *every single year*. In a country of 318 million people, 110 million men and women have a sexually transmitted disease, resulting in direct medical costs of more than 16 billion dollars annually. Half of these new infections occur in young people between the ages of 15 and 24. Sex education, it turns out, is an abysmal failure.[32]

This data is stunning in light of the fact that secular critics deride the teaching of chastity as old-fashioned—something that simply doesn't work anymore. It would seem to be transparently obvious to all those in possession of mental faculties that what has *not* worked is the new sexual anarchy that has been unleashed in the West. For generations, the Judeo-Christian sexual ethic and the elevated social status of the family unit ensured that society could function free of such epidemics. Now the secularists have wrenched the lid of Pandora's Box off its hinges, and claim that it would be pointless to try and put the lid back on. Secularists are difficult to understand at times—they are curiously utopian when it comes to their unflagging belief in man's ability to cure poverty or save the planet from environmental catastrophe. However, when Christians timidly suggest that perhaps young people ought to keep their pants on until marriage, they shriek with outrage at the absurdity of the suggestion. We can control everything, it seems, except ourselves.

And they say Christians are crazy.

The end of marriage

The primary societal casualty of all of this has been the institution of marriage. Contrary to what many Christians might believe, it was not the gay rights activists demanding that marriage be entirely redefined that began the assault on marriage. By then, marriage as an institution that shaped society had already taken a vicious battering. Hook-up culture eliminated marriage as the context for sexual relations. Divorce laws making it easier to opt out of a marriage than a cell phone contract eliminated marriage stability and the need for serious forethought. The hyper-sexualization of virtually every aspect of culture contributes to sky-rocketing rates of infidelity. And aside from that, people are abandoning marriage in droves, seeing it as an unnecessary commitment at a time when they have a variety of relationships open to them.

This will not be news to any reader. Divorce is nearly as common as marriage, and pseudo-marital relationships are even more frequent. Couples can now be sexually active and prevent procreation through contraception or eliminate any resulting children through abortion in order to preserve their independence. They can simply decide to move in with one another without bothering to get married. And if they do get married, they can break it off for any reason or for no reason, regardless of whether or not children are involved. Instead, self-absorbed couples utilize the tragically erroneous excuse that a divorce would be "better for the children." This is nonsense—in fact, nearly every field of study has revealed that the breakdown of the family has resulted in hurting and unhappy children. Focus on the Family, a longstanding opponent of no-fault divorce, compiled one list of the ways divorce impacts children:

> Children from divorced homes suffer academically. They experience high levels of behavioral problems. Their grades suffer, and they are less likely to graduate from high school.
>
> Kids whose parents divorce are substantially more likely to be incarcerated for committing a crime as a juvenile.
>
> Because the custodial parent's income drops substantially after a divorce, children in divorced homes are almost five times more likely to live in poverty than are children with married parents.
>
> Teens from divorced homes are much more likely to engage in drug and alcohol use, as well as sexual intercourse than are those from intact families.
>
> Children from divorced homes experience illness more frequently and recover from sickness more slowly. They are also more likely to suffer child abuse.
>
> Children of divorced parents suffer more frequently from symptoms of psychological distress. And the emotional scars of divorce last into adulthood.[33]

At one time, our culture was largely oriented towards the protection of children. The Sexual Revolution has changed all of that. Besides the physical destruction of the very smallest children through abortion, (which will be covered in Chapter 5,) the collapse of the family structure has created a society in which children are profoundly vulnerable. I cannot count the number of stories teenage girls have told me about falling prey to the new boyfriend of her mother, and the fear these girls have about a strange man moving into their home and often sleeping just down the hall from their bedroom. I can't count the number of conversations I've had with angry, hostile teenage boys and insecure, hurting girls who grew up without fathers. And I think every single one of us knows someone who found themselves alienated and isolated as the result of one or both of their parents entering new marriages and new family arrangements. If pain and heartbreak were measurable, the divorce of parents would be more widely recognized for the cruel tragedy it so often is.

Focus on the Family detailed some of the psychological impacts of divorce:

> Psychologist Judith Wallerstein followed a group of children of divorce from the 1970s into the 1990s. Interviewing them at 18 months and then 5, 10, 15 and 25 years after the divorce, she expected to find that they had bounced back. But what she found was dismaying: Even 25 years after the divorce, these children continued to experience substantial expectations of failure, fear of loss, fear of change and fear of conflict. Twenty-five years!
>
> The children in Wallerstein's study were especially challenged when they began to form their own romantic relationships. As Wallerstein explains, "Contrary to what we have long thought, the major impact of divorce does not occur during childhood or adolescence. Rather, it rises in adulthood as serious romantic relationships move center stage . . . Anxiety leads many [adult children of divorce] into making bad choices in relationships, giving up hastily when problems arise, or avoiding relationships altogether."
>
> As Wallerstein put it, "The kids [in my study] had a hard time remembering the pre-divorce family . . . but what they remembered about the post-divorce years was their sense that they had indeed been abandoned by both parents, that their nightmare [of abandonment] had come true."
>
> Parents tend to want to have their own needs met after a divorce—to find happiness again with someone new. But not only do the old problems often resurface for the adults, new problems are added for the children. As Wallerstein observed, "It's not that parents love their children less or worry less about them. It's that they are fully engaged in rebuilding their own lives — economically, socially and sexually. Parents' and children's needs are often out of sync for many years after the breakup." Children again feel abandoned as parents pursue better relationships after the breakup."[34]

Is it any wonder, then, that a generation of divorced parents has given rise to a generation of adult children deeply afraid of commitment and marriage? Even secular publications have been rendered incredulous by the declining marriage rates—in 2012, *The Atlantic* published an essay detailing the various factors contributing to "the death" of marriage in the United States.

"In 1960, 72% of all adults over 18 were married," the author of the essay noted. "By 2010, the number fell to 51%. You can fault the increase in divorces that peaked in the 1970s. Or you could just blame the twentysomethings. The share of married adults ages 18 to 29 plunged from 59% in 1960 to 20% in 2010. *Twenty percent!*"[35]

In Canada, divorce rates have fluctuated between 35% and 42% since the late 1980s, with the current average settling around 40%—and many Canadians are opting not to get married at all.[36] According to the Government of Canada, "In 2008, there were 147,288 marriages in Canada. At 4.4 marriages per 1,000 people, the marriage rate was at the lowest level it has been in the last century." Those who do get married wait longer than ever before—on average, at age 29 for women and 31 for men.[37]

With the implosion of marriage, the spine of our society is snapping and splintering. Unfortunately, most of the Christian community ignored this disintegration until gay activists began demanding that their relationships, too, be legally recognized as marriages. It was then that the "battle for marriage" began, even though by that time the institution of marriage had been so degraded that the final fight seemed more like a skirmish in the rubble of what once was. The previous battles had already been lost, with the resistance of the churches and political conservatives being, as Peter Hitchens noted, "puny."

"In all Western Christian countries, in the late or middle 1960s," Hitchens told me in another conversation, "laws came into place which meant that if two parties had voluntarily agreed to swear a marriage oath and take part in that, if one of those parties decided to dissolve the marriage and the other wanted to maintain the oath that they'd sworn, the state had the power, ultimately backed by police force and prison, to drag out of the family home the person who wished to abide by the oath and support the person who wished to break it. It was an enormous eruption of state power in the private life. Absolutely devastating, revolutionary beyond all measure."

Revolutionary is precisely right. While redefining marriage to include homosexual relationships may have been symbolic of how firmly Western society had rejected its Judeo-Christian foundation, marriage as a cornerstone of that foundation had been chipped away much earlier. The battle over gay marriage was not actually over marriage, as it turned out. It was over religious liberty and freedom of conscience, a topic that will be covered extensively in Chapter 8.

Chapter 3

The Porn Plague

Pornography's rise to power represents an eruption of evil in truly demonic proportions, as if hell itself were conducting a D-Day operation and had won a beachhead from which to stage a larger invasion.

—Gregg Forster, *First Things*

Porn is everywhere, and porn wrecks everything. Teachers, parents, church leaders, and spouses are just starting to realize this—that just beneath the surface of our society, porn is pervasive.

I live in a quiet subdivision in rural Ontario. I mean very quiet—all summer long, I rarely saw any kids outside biking or playing street hockey or running flimsy lemonade stands or just roughhousing around. Then, the day school started, I was shocked when I left my house in the morning and I saw kids everywhere, backpacks in tow, heading to bus stops and walking to the nearby school. *This many kids live in my neighborhood?* I thought to myself, *Where were they all summer?*

There are a number of possible answers, of course. Some were probably on vacation. Some were probably shipped off to camp by their parents. But many of them were likely inside the house, glued to screens. One recent Canadian overview of child behavior found that "10 to 16 year olds in Canada get an average of 6 hours and 37 minutes of screen time per day. The largest source of screen time is television (2 hours and 39 min) followed by computers (2 hours and 7 min) and video games (1 hour and 51 min)."[38]

The risks apparent in these numbers go far beyond childhood obesity, cyber-bullying, and screens as a substitute for face-to-face interaction. The problem is that many of these children will end up finding and looking at pornography. That pornography will shape the way they view sex as they grow older. Those views will shape how they treat themselves and others. Keep in mind that the average boy, for example, is first exposed to pornography at age eleven. I've even met porn addicts as young as ten.

I speak on sex and pornography in high schools quite often, and every time I do, I'm faced with a dilemma: The adults in the room are likely to be shocked, horrified, and upset when I confront the students with the reality of what online porn is and why it is so dangerous. However, the teenagers, for the most part, are not even remotely shocked. Most of them have seen the things I'm talking about. Increasingly, and chillingly, many have even been coerced or pressured into trying the dark perversions they see unfolding on their tablet, computer, and smartphone screens. It's gotten to the point where I'm relieved when teenagers are shocked by one of my presentations—it means that they've heard the information in time to avoid the clutching webs of the Internet porn industry.

I'm quite often accused of being an alarmist by parents and church leaders who can't quite believe just how pervasive porn use and porn exposure is among the very young. I'm often told that this is the reason that having a presentation on pornography would be "too controversial." Quite frankly, I wish they were right. But consider just a few of these current statistics, publicized by the anti-porn organization Covenant Eyes in 2014:

> 35% of teen boys say they have viewed pornographic videos "more times than they can count."
>
> 15% of boys and 9% of girls *have seen child pornography.*
>
> 32% of boys and 18% of girls *have seen bestiality online.*
>
> 39% of boys and 23% of girls *have seen sexual bondage online.*
>
> 83% of boys and 57% of girls *have seen group sex online.*

In addition to that, 64% to 68% of young adult men and about 18% of women confess to using pornography *at least once every single week*. Another 17% of men and another 30% of women use pornography at least one or two times every single month. What does this mean? It means that 85% of young men and 48% of young women are using pornography every single month. Today, if you're not looking at pornography, you're in the minority. And it starts young.[*39]

I've met more teens than I can count whose first exposure to porn—and not just "normal" porn but dark, violent porn that is now mainstream—was at the ages of ten or eleven. I've met parents who tell me how relieved they are that their children never had a porn problem, when I've spoken to their children and I know that their children did, in fact, struggle with porn. After one presentation, I even had an anonymous letter sent to me by a wife and mother who revealed that throughout my presentation on pornography, she felt relieved that her husband would never look at such things. She found out a short time later that he had been looking at pornography for a long time.

I'm not being alarmist when I say that this problem is everywhere. It's a grim fact.

Some time ago, for example, I spoke at a high school conference for Christian schools. One of the things I like to do to show the teachers and other adults just how essential it is to provide teens with the truth about pornography is to hold an open forum—let the students write down any and all questions they have about the topic and submit them to be answered. Every time, teachers are shocked by what the students are asking as they realize just how far this menace has spread and how badly it has infected our schools.

At one conference, I had a fourteen-year-old girl ask me what girls should do when their boyfriends pressure them into anal sex (hugely popular in mainstream porn right now.) I had teen boys asking me how to deal with their masturbation problems. I was asked why porn sites were so addicting. I was asked by

* For consistently up-to-date statistics, visit covenanteyes.com

one girl why so many boys were demanding oral sex. And I was even asked questions about bestiality in porn, questions even I had a hard time believing teens of that age could be asking.

Porn impacts all relationships

I read a column from Anthony Esolen called "What they will never know" a few years back, and he beautifully highlights what the teens of today are being robbed of: "Our teenagers who know so much about the mechanics of copulation miss the sweetness of simple humanity. People used to sing merrily about holding a girl's hand while walking home...holding a hand. With that touch, they knew the thrill, perhaps for the first time, of being deemed worthy of love. What is it like, to be a boy or a girl who could be made dizzyingly happy by so simple a touch? We will never know."

It's very true. And it's one of the reasons I ended up getting involved in anti-porn work. I was never particularly passionate about the issue—I figured that it didn't impact my life much. Sure, porn was a big problem. But not in my sphere. Not with my friends. I didn't clue in for quite some time that pornography was extraordinarily pervasive—not even when one of my university professors brought up the topic of porn, and in the entire class, only me and one other guy were opposed to it. Everyone else defended pornography as either a good thing or as a "freedom."

But one by one, I started finding out that many of my friends had looked at porn. Some were still looking at porn. In many cases, had been looking at pornography for years, and from very young ages. I began to realize, with a sickening feeling, that those who hadn't been exposed to pornography at a very young age or those who had managed to successfully avoid it were very much an aberration. We are the Porn Generation. It is everywhere. It seems like the more stories I hear, the more people come forward with new stories.

I remember one afternoon vividly. I was sitting in a truck after one of my pro-life presentations. The sobbing middle-aged husband and father in the driver's seat was telling me that he had been addicted to porn for over ten years—and that no matter what he tried, he couldn't kick the habit.

Here was a successful businessman, a thoughtful Christian, a husband of a wonderful woman and a father of beautiful girls. He had every reason to stay away from porn—and in spite of all of that, the acidic tentacles of Internet pornography constantly pulled him in, over and over again.

The realization made me feel sick. How many fathers feel distant from their children because they are watching girls the same age as their daughters do horrifying and degrading things and having those things done to them? How many husbands feel disconnected from their wives because they've watched thousands of air-brushed, naked women pass before their eyes on the screen of their computer?

Worse, I wondered, how must these women feel when they discover what their husbands and boyfriends are doing? How must a wife feel when her husband confesses his porn addiction? As feminist writer Naomi Wolf noted, "Here is what young women tell me on college campuses when the subject comes up: They can't compete, and they know it...Today, real naked women are just bad porn."[40]

That encounter was one of the many reasons I got involved in the fight against pornography.

That is why, when a friend emailed me an article showing how pornography has contributed enormously to the collapse of marriages, I wasn't surprised. According to the research, in 56% of divorces one of the parties has an obsessive interest in Internet pornography.[41]

And that makes perfect sense: I know that women these days are supposed to pretend that they are enlightened enough to accept the presence of thousands of other nude women in their relationships. Otherwise they might be considered "prudish." But as porn researchers such as Pamela Paul (author of *Pornified: How Pornography Is Damaging Our Lives, Our Relationships, and Our Families*) have found, the presence of porn inevitably leads to jealousy, insecurity, and a damaged relationship.

Pornography isn't just destroying marriages and relationships. It's rewiring our brains to create hypersexual people incapable of enjoying many of the simple joys of family life. For example, one of the things I like to do after a long week at work is to go to my parents' place and hang out with my family. My youngest sister is eleven, and we snuggle on the couch and she tells me all about her day, and what she's doing in school, and about her cats, and other things eleven-year-old girls think about. It's a special time, and one of the best parts of my weekend. That's why one email I got from a young man, who is thankfully now free of pornography, was so painful for me to read:

> How did porn impact my life? I became extremely callous. I now do not feel how I think I should feel. I am not empathetic. I wasted two years of my life trying to find ways to get more pornography without anyone knowing. I committed adultery in my heart with more women than I care to count. That leaves scar tissue.
>
> A big problem is with physical affection. I have trouble not sexualizing everything out of the ordinary (a greeting hug vs. a random hug). It has been noted that I am more physically affectionate with my friends than my sisters. That is because I feel no attraction to men whatsoever, so it isn't sexual to me.
>
> I am more sexually knowledgeable and aware than I think I have any right to be.

It isn't just a marriage that can be destroyed by pornography. Pornography is a poison that can seep through a whole family. Another young man emailed me some time ago, writing:

> I was exposed to hard-core porn around 11 years old; it was my father's (who was/is a pastor) and was hidden in my basement. My older brother showed it to me and warned me that I couldn't share any of this with our parents because it could lead to them breaking up.

I find these emails difficult to read. I was blessed with a happy home and a happy childhood. I spent my time reading books or playing outdoors, hiding in a culvert catching frogs, playing with our family dog, making half-finished tree forts, or hatching elaborate scenarios to play out with my siblings. My childhood wasn't scarred by images too searing and too perverse to comprehend or compute. I was allowed to experience innocence. And that's because our home was porn-free.

Porn wrecks marriages

In millions of homes, pornography is an insidious influence impacting every aspect of family life, and women are being forced to compete with pornography for the attention of their husbands. One of our culture's great lies is that porn can "help a marriage"—and that it can actually assist in marital intimacy. Besides the fact that the delusional idea of introducing other naked people into a marriage is a wicked and adulterous one, the facts and statistics do not bear this assertion out. Quite the opposite.

For example, Covenant Eyes cited in their 2014 statistics a number of conclusions reached by the *Journal of Adolescent Health* about the impact of pornography:

- An exaggerated perception of sexual activity in society
- Diminished trust between intimate couples
- The abandonment of the hope of sexual monogamy
- Belief that promiscuity is the natural state
- Belief that abstinence and sexual inactivity are unhealthy
- Cynicism about love or the need for affection between sexual partners
- Belief that marriage is sexually confining
- Lack of attraction to family and child-raising[42]

This should not, of course, be particularly surprising. The fact that watching thousands of other people having sex, or at least some sterile, pornified fantasy version of intercourse, would be poisonous to the idea of fully committing oneself to another for life would seem to be an easy conclusion to reach. One woman wrote to me that when she first found out about her husband's porn struggles, she was devastated: "I was too shocked to respond. Once that wore off I experienced much anger, low self-esteem, sadness, and insecurity about our relationship."

Often, these feelings culminate in divorce. One woman, writing anonymously, published a heartbreaking autopsy of her marriage in the left-wing newspaper, *The Guardian*. She was very liberal, she writes, very "open-minded," even. But at the end of the day, pornography destroyed her marriage:

> Porn ruined you. Ruined us. When people asked, shocked, how I could leave such a funny, clever man, father of my children—"a good earner" as my mother put it—what could I say? I said it was me. My fault. I'd changed. Only it wasn't me. It was your love of porn that slowly diminished my love and respect for you and destroyed my self-confidence. I couldn't tell them and I've never said it straight to you but you must know, you must remember those conversations. The rows…
>
> We were about six months in when I found your stash and I picked it up smiling—"Boys will be boys"—expecting Penthouse Pets, Readers' Wives etc. but found women so mutilated by beach-ball, supersize-me, fake breasts that their eyes registered pain where their pouts pretended otherwise.
>
> I felt it was mutilation. I wept. You shrugged off my arguments—"They get paid. It's their choice"—and dismissed my arguments about exploitation as unchecked radical feminism.
>
> So why did I stay? In the rest of our life you were funny, left-wing, Mr. PC, cultured, creative; and we could talk forever about politics, 70s sitcoms, obscure 80s bands … Anyway, like the frog in the slowly heating water I didn't realise or I'd have jumped out…

> And, I told myself, sex isn't everything, is it? Not when everything else is so right. I thought maybe, in time, we would learn together, maybe you will connect the emotion with the action. I tried to explain how it could be, but could only conclude that your lack of desire for sex with me was my fault...
>
> What came next was not easy. Tears, guilt, divorce, kids shuttled between two homes, the shockwaves to extended family and friends. I'm in a relationship now...
>
> You are still alone. People think it's because you haven't moved on. That you're still in love with me. But I think it's because relationships require effort and consideration of other's needs, and the women you spend most of your time with ask for nothing. You are actually happier in your relationship with porn.[43]

The idea that porn would help a marriage is obscenely laughable. Covenant Eyes, in their 2014 report on the effects of pornography, laid out in great detail the various effects of porn use on marriages and relationships:

> According to sociologist Jill Manning, the research indicates pornography consumption is associated with the following six trends, among others:
>
> 1. Increased marital distress, and risk of separation and divorce
>
> 2. Decreased marital intimacy and sexual satisfaction
>
> 3. Infidelity
>
> 4. Increased appetite for more graphic types of pornography and sexual activity associated with abusive, illegal or unsafe practices
>
> 5. Devaluation of monogamy, marriage and child rearing
>
> 6. An increasing number of people struggling with compulsive and addictive sexual behavior

In 2002, the American Academy of Matrimonial Lawyers reported the following as the most salient factors present in divorce cases:

68% of the divorces involved one party meeting a new lover over the Internet.

56% involved one party having "an obsessive interest in pornographic websites."

47% involved spending excessive time on the computer.

33% involved excessive time spent speaking in chat rooms.

In a survey of women (and some men) who experienced serious adverse consequences from their partner's cybersex involvement:

In 68% of the couples, one or both lost interest in relational sex

52% of showed a decreased interest, as did 34% of partners.

Partners commonly reported feeling hurt, betrayed, rejected, abandoned, lonely, isolated, humiliated, jealous, and angry. Partners often compared themselves unfavorably to online images. Partners overwhelmingly felt that cyber affairs were as emotionally painful as offline affairs.

In a survey of 63 wives of self-identified sex addicts:

70% met most criteria for a diagnosis of post-traumatic stress disorder.

75% discovered evidence of compulsive or addictive sexual behaviors themselves (as opposed to a planned disclosure on the part of a husband).

71% demonstrated a severe level of functional impairment in major areas of their lives.

Length of marriage at disclosure and number of prior traumatic event exposures were the best predictors of increased trauma symptoms.[44]

This trend is why advice columns in publications of every sort explode with women asking how they should deal with their husband's pornography use. Many of them want to oppose it—at least 34% of women still see viewing porn as cheating in all cases—but they're not sure how.[45] Many of them feel, Pamela Paul writes in *Pornified,* that "admitting they don't look at pornography at all is akin to affixing a 'frigid' sticker to their chastity belts; better not to come off as uptight."[46]

Women resent the presence of pornography in their marriage, but in many cases, feel helpless to fight it in a culture where porn is virtually accepted as a regular part of life. Even women's magazines, Paul writes, "have regularly featured a discussion of pornography from a new perspective: how women can introduce it into their own lives. While many women continue to have mixed or negative feelings towards pornography, they are told to be realistic, to be 'open-minded.' Porn, they are told, is sexy, and if you want to be a sexually attractive and forward-thinking woman, you've got to catch on."[47]

Many women hate pornography because they know that it changes the way men look at them. "According to the [nationally representative] *Pornified*/Harris poll," Pamela Paul writes, "most women (six out of ten) believe pornography affects how men expect them to look and behave. In fact, only 15 percent of women believe that pornography *does not* raise men's expectations."[48]

Pornography doesn't simply "raise expectations," it fundamentally changes the way the genders relate to one another. Pornography portrays women as objects of male pleasure, and promotes the view that women exist for the satisfaction of men. Paul theorizes that it is sexual frustration that drives men to watch porn—but that is very revealing, as it insinuates that many men have already adopted the view that women are objects on which to release sexual frustration in the first place, rather than life partners, spouses to love and cherish.

Girls watch porn, too

One of the biggest stories surrounding the explosive growth of the porn industry over the past two decades is the enormous numbers of girls and women who are now addicted to porn, as well. And not just the Harlequins and smutty books that were once marketed as the first so-called "mommy porn," but brutal videos, bizarre sex scenes, and hard-core porn.

While men are still 543% more likely to consume pornography on a regular basis than women are, the gap is slowly closing.[49] Pornography, traditionally regarded as a "male sin," is no longer that: 32% of females viewed porn before the age of 12, 18% of females use porn at least once a week, and 49% of women say viewing porn is an acceptable expression of sexuality.[50] In my first year of university when my political science professor asked the class who was opposed to pornography and who was for it, it was only myself and one other male student who admitted to opposing pornography. Female students were the porn industry's most strident defenders.

One female friend, after hearing a porn presentation I gave, came to talk to me. "You need to mention the fact that girls struggle with this too," she said. A few days later, she emailed me her story:

> I've battled addiction to masturbation for as long as I can remember. All the groundwork for my porn addiction had already been laid.
>
> But the actual progression to porn was a gradual one. It began with reading sexually explicit passages from romance novels that belonged to my mom and were shouting at me from the top of the bookshelf. Those stories weren't quite graphic enough however, and I thought I found what I wanted when I found *Cosmopolitan* magazines under my sister's bed. I devoured all the '101 Mind-blowing Sex Tips' and sex stories, laying my hands on all the material I could find. I thought it was quite graphic at the time, but it filled my appetite, if only for a while.
>
> It wasn't until I got my first smartphone, with access to Wi-Fi, that I really tried to find porn. I had absolutely no idea what I would find. Having opened that door—no,

> that floodgate—I now wish I never had.
>
> I was blown away by the variety of porn out there. I perused the never ending categories, being disturbed by some but mostly titillated by the unknown and the immense adrenaline and arousal I felt. I quickly developed preferences and knew exactly what I would like within seconds of starting a video.

She explained how porn began to give her fantasies about being abused and disrespected, and how the hatred and contempt for women that came through in the mainstream porn she consumed impacted the way she thought. Now married with children, her past pornography use still impacts her in many ways, and like all recovering porn addicts, the battle to stay away from the poison goes on.

Personalized pornography

There's also the phenomenon of "sexting"—here, too, both genders seem to be participating with equal enthusiasm. *Slate.com* noted that while the rates of boys and girls sexting—specifically, sending nude pictures of themselves—are pretty much the same, boys are far more likely to send these pictures on to their peers, resulting in often savage bullying that has culminated in tragedies like the recent suicides of several young girls.

Sexting was not really a phenomenon when I was in high school, as the cell phones we used weren't advanced enough to facilitate that kind of behavior. But when two of my colleagues and I were meeting with a group of high school students who had expressed interest in getting involved spreading the pro-life message inside their high schools, they soon informed us of how quickly the trend was spreading.

One of them mentioned, almost off-handedly, that the pressure on girls to send explicit pictures was constant. "They keep asking until you give in," she told us. Wondering just how pervasive this phenomenon was, I sent a series of emails around asking various students whether or not that was true—

and what sort of impact that had on the high school culture. What makes their responses even more shocking, I think, is the fact that all of these students attend either Catholic schools or private Protestant schools.

"I find that those who sext because of peer pressure or because they are trying to keep someone interested are most often young girls," one girl responded. "I'm not saying boys don't receive the same pressure from friends, but I find that it is most often the girl's job to keep the boys interested, and what better way than to show them exactly what they want to see? In those cases of peer pressure or those of keeping someone interested, the people who had sexted most often tried to hide it. What always seems to happen, though, is that the people who receive the initial picture show it to all of their friends. Eventually rumors spread, and friendships are ruined and people are hurt in the process. It's things like this that cause teenagers to hurt themselves or commit suicide."

Dr. Arthur Cassidy, a social psychologist commenting on the "sexting" phenomenon in *The Guardian*, agrees: "I think it's most dominant in young girls. Many more girls buy glossy magazines than boys, and there are more female sexually explicit icons. Statistically you also get more attention [on online social networking sites] if you put up a photo of yourself and the more explicit the photo, the more responses you get…Females have more sexual pressure on them now than ever before, so rather than focus on the inner person, it's about looking at the body as a sexual image."[51]

That, of course, is the root of the problem: "It's about looking at the body as a sexual image." A thing, not a person. An object to be desired, not a friend to be made. Another high school student wrote that a huge number of boys in her classes were viewing pornography every night. When they arrive at school, of course, many boys are no longer satisfied with forming intellectual friendships with their female peers—they want to objectify them in the same way they objectify the faceless parade of porn stars they viewed the evening before. They want personalized pornography, a brand new sexual high. High school girls are pressured into thinking that in order to keep and maintain male attention, they have to provide the very tools the boys will use to objectify them and render them faceless.

"To be honest I was kind of happy he texted," Cassie* wrote to me in an email, "At least someone was thinking about me. We talked about everything from dogs to push-ups. He asked me to send him a picture. I'm not stupid and I know what he meant, but I asked him what he wanted a picture of. This is where I should have drawn the line or perhaps even earlier. I know that now and did then too but didn't particularly care. He slowed my phone down by sending me hundreds of megabytes' worth of pictures taken of his bare stomach and groin. I laughed. I don't know why. He asked for a picture again. I sent him one of my face. His next comment was a long exaggerated 'nooooooooo not that' and then 'you made a little mistake' (another smiley) 'I'll give you another chance.' I then walked up a flight of stairs, went inside the bathroom, angrily took my clothes off, snapped two pictures exactly, and sent them."

Sent, and irretrievable. Everything about this interaction shows what is actually at play in much of the gender dynamics surrounding sexting. He asked for a picture—she was "not stupid, and knew what he was asking for." She sent one of her face—and, revealingly, that was precisely what this boy did *not* want. He didn't want to see *her*; he wanted to see her body. The eyes may be the window to the soul, but that's not the type of connection he was after. Rather, he was seeking something much more carnivorous—one-sided pleasure at her expense. And, thinking that "at least someone was thinking about me," she complied. (The subtle social coercion in the underlying threat of "I'll give you another chance" is unmistakable.) It does not take a social scientist to see that while there are two guilty parties involved in this transaction, exploiting the insecurities of females in a hyper-sexualized culture for sexual gratification is, at best, predatory. And while girls are most certainly part of the problem, it is the girls, most often (just as in so-called "recreational" sex), that pay the highest price.

---

* Names have been changed to protect the privacy of contributors.

That reality impacts the high school culture even subliminally. "It's hard to walk into school every day knowing that people there had seen something they never should have, knowing that it would be almost impossible to live it down, forget it and move on," Lindsay told me, "You'd always get smirks and snide comments, shouts in the middle of class or in the cafeteria, even in the hallways walking from place to place. You'd see it all over Facebook, comments you know couldn't be about anyone else. You wouldn't be able to just leave your problems at school because they would follow you home. It's terrible what one little mistake can do to your life. And it's worse that there are even demands for pictures still, after all that has happened to other teens because of it. I don't think these teenagers realize how much this can affect their lives and the lives of the other people involved."

Searching for self-esteem and whatever they define as "love," girls are increasingly collaborating with our culture's attempt to reduce them to sex objects in the vain hope that it will bring them what they're looking for. If "sexting" brings them the attention they crave, many mistakenly think that it's the type of attention that will be fulfilling. As Richelle wrote, "When they are asked to participate in that, they don't think twice because someone is finally 'valuing' them and showing interest in them. They use it as a Band-Aid solution to what they are dealing with because reaching out to others seems to have failed."

From music videos to "teen" magazines, to Hollywood films and TV shows targeted towards their age groups, girls are being conditioned to think that their physical appearance is what gives them value as people. Probably (I hope) without even realizing it, the boys are taking advantage of this cultural conditioning by requesting—and in many, many cases receiving—the personalized pornography that they seek.

The problem of sexting seems to be a hard one to address, in spite of the fact that several high-profile bullying cases resulting in suicide have highlighted the problem and oh-so-briefly outraged the public. Teenage sub-culture is hard for adults to penetrate, especially since teens are now connected to each other via the Internet and cell phones without any adult oversight. One girl warned me that, "If you're trying to change the minds of teenagers with this information, it probably won't work." And there's probably a lot of truth to that. Especially when requests for explicit pictures stem from pornography addictions, it's going to take a lot to convince teenagers in high schools that this behavior is self-destructive, demeaning, and an attack on the dignity (self-inflicted though it often may be) of the girls sending the photos, as well as the boys receiving them.

As Covenant Eyes has revealed, these practices are a lot more common than parents, educators, and church leaders would suspect:

> 4% of 12 year olds have sent a sext.
>
> 7% of 14 to 17 year olds have sent a sext.
>
> 9% of 13 to 18 year olds have sent a sext.
>
> 19% of 18 to 24 year olds have sent a sext.
>
> According to a 2013 ChildLine poll of 500 children in the UK, ages 13 to 18:
>
> 60% said they have been asked for explicit photos or videos of themselves. 38% said they had created a sext. Of these, 32% said they had sent it to someone they knew online only (not in real life).
>
> Of those who sent a sext, 20% said it had been shared with others, and 28% said they did not know if it was shared.
>
> 8% of 14 to 24 year olds have participated in a webcam chat during which someone else performed sexual activities.
>
> When 535 students from 18 schools in South West UK responded to a survey, nearly 4 out of 10 said at least one of their friends has "shared intimate pictures/videos" with a boyfriend or girlfriend.
>
> Sexting can be a precursor to virtual slander. Among 14 to 24 year olds, 10% say that someone had sent them

> naked pictures or videos of someone else that they know personally, while 13% said someone had showed them similar pictures.[52]

The prevalence of sexting and personalized pornography has followed closely on the heels of Internet pornography's rise. The new gender dynamics created by pornography mean that to many boys and men, every girl and every woman is a potential porn star. All it takes is a bit of persuasion.

Revenge porn

"Revenge porn" is different from the sexting phenomenon, although the two are inextricably linked. Since sending nude or semi-nude photos is now the norm in relationships, people —especially women and girls—are finding themselves in the uncomfortable position of exiting relationships with those who have in their possession extremely intimate photographs. Angry ex-partners, in turn, are often spreading these photos far and wide—either to a group of friends via social networks, by mass-forwarding it on to others, or, in some cases, sending the images to "revenge porn" websites (which exist solely for the purpose of hosting these images and ruining people's lives.) Many of these sites include the victim's name, address, and social networks. Some revenge porn sites even blackmail their victims by offering them "reputation protection"—the removal of their images in exchange for a large fee. The intent is to objectify, humiliate, and destroy.

Porn culture and the digital age, meet the jilted lover.

Fortunately, action is being taken against this new trend, slowly but surely. Nine states, including California, Utah, and New Jersey, have all passed laws against it. Some include jail time. Israel made the distribution of revenge porn a sex crime punishable by jail, with one Knesset member calling it "virtual rape." The German High Court has ruled that ex-partners must delete such photos upon demand. And in Canada, legislators have recently put forward a cyber-bullying bill that includes up to five years of jail-time for anyone publishing pornographic photos online of someone they know.

Porn causes sexual dysfunction

The reality is that pornography does not just cause perverse and dysfunctional sexual behavior, but also causes sexual dysfunction itself. Mainstream headlines are increasingly taking note of this. *Porn causing erectile dysfunction in young men,* warned *Global News. Internet pornography destroying men's ability to perform with real women,* announced the *Daily Mail. Does porn contribute to erectile dysfunction?* asked *Psychology Today.*

The short answer is: yes, it does. Let me illustrate with one powerful example.

Hugh Hefner, the founder of the Playboy empire, has been idolized by millions of men of dubious morals for his lifestyle—his huge mansion, never-ending stream of celebrity guests, and, of course, the girls. He is considered the ultimate playboy, the silk-pajamaed icon of the Sexual Revolution, the man who brought "free love" to the free market and made a fortune.

He's also sexually dysfunctional.

In her emotionally mauling book *Pornland: How Porn Has Hijacked Our Sexuality,* researcher Gail Dines writes how the infamous TV show "The Girls Next Door," which started in 2005, "provides a sanitized version of life at the Playboy mansion, never showing the reality of the experiences for the young women who live and sleep with eighty-three-year-old Hefner."[53]

Perhaps most revealingly, she points out how Izabella St. James, one of Hefner's 'ex-girlfriends,' has written that while Hefner would often have unprotected sex with multiple women, he could not reach sexual completion without using pornography and stimulating himself.

Porn is reducing millions of men to pathetic dependents desperately scrolling through thousands of pictures and videos—and causing many of them to become impotent. Even a man with a non-stop stream of beautiful women sleeping with him, one of the most easily recognizable sex icons of our time, cannot get off without porn. The Porn Generation's very own Marlboro Man.

Like thirsty men and women guzzling salt water, we simply inflame our lusts with pornography, dehydrating ourselves of the true human intimacy we crave. Porn functions like a drug—and rather than helping the sex lives of those who use it, it actually destroys real intimacy, just as it destroys marriages, replacing them with cyber-fantasy.

Marnia Robinson, who co-authored *Cupid's Poisoned Arrow: Biology Has Plans for Your Love Life* with her husband Dr. Wilson, explained this phenomenon. LifeSiteNews reported on her findings:

> Robinson explains that the brain can become desensitized to dopamine, the neurotransmitter that activates the body's reaction to sexual pleasure, through the kind of over-stimulation readily available via the Internet's porn culture.
>
> The result is that users fall into a chemical dependency, requiring larger doses to achieve the same effect. This phenomenon drives the market for "extreme genres" of porn and decreases an addict's ability to respond to real life sexual encounters.
>
> "It's all free, easy to access, available within seconds, 24 hours a day, 7 days a week. Overstimulation of the reward circuitry in the brain is a very real possibility today," Robinson explains. "Many men don't realize their brain's sensitivity is declining toward normal sex because Internet erotica delivers endless dopamine hits."
>
> Men who have attempted to stop a pornography addiction report withdrawal symptoms such as temporary drop in libido, insomnia, irritability, panic, despair, concentration problems, and even flu-like symptoms.[54]

Pornography, far from being the "sex aid" many attempt to claim it is, actually destroys both intimacy and sex.

Porn is a drug

There is one very simple reason that pornography is so destructive, so pervasive, and so powerful: Pornography functions like a drug.

This really should come as no surprise to anyone. Simply listen to how people describe their struggles with porn—it is the language of addiction. People talk about staying "clean" for a period of time. They discuss how they are "struggling" with porn, but that they've "lapsed" or "backslidden" recently. They highlight all the various barriers they've had to place between themselves and sources of pornography, to prevent them from logging on and using porn again.

All addictions flourish because of the Triple-A combination: affordability, accessibility, and anonymity. Pornography today easily fulfills all three. There is a vast assortment of free porn on the Internet. It is accessible from virtually every type of technological device, from your cell phone to your computer to your iPad. And you can do it in complete privacy. Twenty or thirty years ago, looking at porn was quite a process. You'd have to sneak out to an X-rated theatre late at night, all the while taking precautions so that no one would see you. Or as I only half-jokingly told one radio host asking me about the porn plague, not so long ago you'd have to don a hat and trench coat, slink to the back of the corner store while everyone nodded knowingly, buy your carefully wrapped magazine or video while everyone in the store judged you, and slink back out of the store. Nowadays, all you need is a few spare minutes and your cell phone, and you can access the most depraved and bizarre material known to humankind.

This addiction, like any drug addiction, changes the brain in dangerous ways. Not only do porn addicts need harder and more extreme pornography featuring increasingly disturbing sex acts to "get off" or attain the high, porn also starts to permanently rewire our brain. Matt Fradd of The Porn Effect writes:

> The brain is designed in such a way to respond to sexual stimulation. Surges of dopamine are released

> during a sexual encounter—and yes, also pornographic encounters—giving the person a sharp sense of focus and an awareness of sexual craving. Dopamine helps to lay down memories in the brain, so the next time a man or woman is in the mood, the brain remembers where to return to experience the same pleasure: whether that be a loving spouse or the laptop in the den.
>
> However, scientists are now seeing that continued exposure to porn gives the brain an unnatural high—something it literally isn't wired to handle—and the brain eventually fatigues. Anatomy and physiology instructor Gary Wilson notes this is the same pattern noticed when drugs are abused: the brain becomes desensitized. More of the drug or harder drugs are needed to get the same high, and the downward spiral begins. Wilson says this brings about significant changes in the brain—both for drug abusers and porn users.
>
> One of those changes is the erosion of the prefrontal cortex—that all-important center of executive control. When this region of the brain is weakened, when the craving for porn hits, there is very little willpower present to regulate the desire. Neuroscientists call this problem hypofrontality, where the person slowly loses impulse control and the mastery of his or her passions.[55]

Just as someone who began their journey into the world of drug addiction with cannabis can eventually proceed onwards into cocaine, heroin, and crystal meth, so too can a fascination with "soft-core" pornography or sexual imagery eventually evolve into something much darker and far more gruesome.

This is the future of the porn industry. And if we don't do something about it, this is the future of our society. For as Dr. James B. Weaver noted, "In men, prolonged exposure to pornography creates and enhances sexual callousness toward women [...] Prolonged exposure to pornography, it must be remembered, results in both a loss of respect for female sexual autonomy and the disinhibition of men in the expression of aggression against women."[56]

How could it not? Every industry is now using hypersexualized imagery of women and girls to push every imaginable product, and images of acts of depravity that would have been unthinkable mere decades ago have become mainstream. Pornography is a poison, and our society is drinking it very, very deeply.

Chapter 4

The Rape Culture Everyone is Ignoring

Amateurs come across better on screen. Our customers feel that. Especially by women you can see it. They still feel strong pain.

—Carlo Scalisi, owner of the porn company 21 Sexury Video

What is rape culture?

Does "rape culture" exist? The very suggestion usually invites loud shouting from all sides of the political spectrum. Anyone who pays attention to the news will have noticed that the phrase "rape culture" is growing in prominence, as mainstream media sources constantly refer to an explosion of sexual assault on university campuses as being indicative of "rape culture."

Originating as a rather marginal concept pushed by the radical feminist set in the 1970s, "rape culture" was, essentially, an accusation leveled by feminist activists against the United States and its male citizens. America, they said, was a nation where rape was prevalent. This, of course, pointed to a country suffering from deep-seated misogyny and an enormous number of rapists, lending dubious credence to the man-hating claims of some radical feminists while supporting the claim of many conservatives that "feminist" actually meant "anti-men." Books such as *Rape: The First Sourcebook for Women* released in 1974 and Susan Brownmiller's *Against Our Will: Men, Women, and Rape* released in 1975 utilized chilling first-hand accounts of rape to drive home their point.

Today, however, "rape culture" is being used to describe rising rates of sexual assault on university campuses across

North America. Several members of the men's hockey team at the University of Ottawa were recently accused of sexual assault, while a student leader revealed that in a Facebook conversation, several male student leaders had made sexually explicit comments about her with one comment stating that she should be "sexually punished." These events harkened back to incidents in 2013 at St. Mary's University, where a frosh-week chant featured male students chanting support for non-consensual, underage sex—"U is for underage! N is for no consent!"—and a variety of other disgusting and explicit lyrics. Similar events have occurred across the United States, prompting even President Barack Obama and Vice-President Joe Biden to speak out and create a "House Task Force to Protect Students from Sexual Assault." Some research has suggested that one in five women in university report being sexually assaulted. Those numbers are stomach-churning to say the very least.

The existence of a "rape culture" on university campuses has been much debated, with some commentators claiming that sexual assault numbers are being very much inflated while warning against convicting alleged rapists without due process. The response to these doubts have been a combination of hysterical accusations of "victim-blaming" and more measured voices highlighting heartbreaking stories of brutal rapes being dismissed by university officials, including a female student at Columbia University who promised to carry her mattress around campus with her until her rapist was expelled. It's hard to separate the cold hard data from the emotionally-charged din surrounding the discussion, but one thing is certain: As hook-up culture and unprecedented binge drinking collide on campuses, the result is yet another tragic manifestation of a very broken sexual culture.

That's the rape culture that our society *is* talking about. What I want to expose in this chapter is the rape culture that *almost no one* is talking about.

This rape culture is more insidious because very few voices are addressing it, and it is rapidly impacting huge numbers of young people across North America with devastating results.

It is a rape culture emanating from the glowing screens of cell phones, iPads, laptops, and television sets, and it is one of the greatest threats to the upcoming generation: Pornography.

Pornography is creating a rape culture

In the last chapter I laid out many of the adverse effects of pornography and examined how porn use and porn addiction are so widespread that our culture is reaching the saturation point. This viral manifestation of the Sexual Revolution has left virtually no home untouched. But unfortunately, it gets much, much worse. Pornography is fueling a new rape culture, wiring the trivialization of sexual assault right into our cultural psyche.

I realize that this thesis incurs a lot of skepticism. I've spoken on this topic all across Canada, including the University of Ottawa and the University of Toronto. *Come on,* people tell me with an earnest "lighten up" tone, *pornography is harmless. And the women in porn love sex, it's why they chose that career.*

Conservatives have a tendency to inform me that "rape culture" is a feminist myth, and therefore all arguments that I put forward using that framework are a non-starter. Liberals and porn-defenders tend to grow hysterical, insisting that the girls being beaten up in violent porn movies enjoy the abuse thoroughly, although they never even begin to explain how.

(I believe there is an interesting reason behind this. The defenders of uninhibited sexual "freedom" are beginning to realize that if we can question the morality of some types of sexual behavior, no matter how abusive and depraved, we can then start questioning other types of sexual behavior as well. Relativism must be maintained at all costs, or the whole bloody experiment of the Sexual Revolution may come crashing down like the shoddily constructed house of cards it is.)

Both the conservatives and the liberals, if indeed they can be shoved into such categories, are tragically wrong in this instance. Consider this: Rape culture has a variety of definitions, but all of them include the basic concept that rape culture can develop when "prevalent attitudes and practices normalize, excuse, tolerate, and even condone rape." Examples of this behavior, to continue quoting, are "victim blaming, sexual objectification, and trivializing rape." Pornography has created a rape culture because it normalizes rape, increases toleration for rape, sexually objectifies women, and absolutely, undoubtedly *trivializes* rape.

THE DUKE UNIVERSITY PORN STAR

Let me start with an example. One of the prime examples of how much female porn stars apparently love being in the porn industry in 2014 was the much-touted "Duke University Porn Star," an eighteen-year-old girl named Miriam Weeks who revealed, much to the university's chagrin, that she was starring in porn films to pay for her tuition. Weeks was the porn industry's perfect cover girl, a Catholic school graduate who freed herself from the totalitarian sexual ideology of her parents to revel gleefully in all the fruits of the Sexual Revolution that had previously been denied her. She was definitive proof that porn was not harmful—and it was fun, too! Miriam Weeks, who goes by the porn handle "Belle Knox," even stated in one interview that, "My experience in porn has been nothing but supportive, exciting, thrilling, and empowering. For me, shooting pornography brings me unimaginable joy…It is my artistic outlet, my happiness, my home." She went on to describe pornography as "freeing, it is empowering, it is wonderful, it is how the world should be."

Some "rape culture," right? An eighteen-year-old freed from the confines of traditional sexual morality has not been abused, she has been freed and empowered!

That narrative came brutally crashing down when former porn star Shelley Lubben of the Pink Cross Foundation released a video featuring Weeks, with the nudity blurred out, being savagely beaten by a muscular male porn star. LifeSiteNews reported the story:

> Former porn star Shelley Lubben of the Pink Cross Foundation has now posted a graphic video showing a male pornographic actor repeatedly choking, slapping, shaking, and verbally abusing Weeks…

> "How does it make you feel personally to, like, watch degrading sex or see women being degraded and treated like s—t or just objectified?" a male interviewer asks Weeks.
>
> "Hot as h***," Weeks replied.
>
> A muscular actor then grabs her around the throat as she fights to loosen his grip around her larynx. After learning she describes herself as a feminist, the man slaps her numerous times, telling her she is worthless.
>
> As a trail of moisture trickles from her eyes down her haggard face, he says, "Feminism 101 right here," before continuing his assault.[57]

Regardless of whether or not that porn shoot was consensual—and in interviews with many people from the porn industry, I have discovered that girls are often coerced or manipulated into these situations—I think we can all agree that watching an eighteen-year old girl get choked, slapped, and beaten up by a verbally abusive male is not "empowering," or "wonderful," and is certainly not "the way the world should be." It is vile and creepy to consider that many, many men are now using such porn films for sexual satisfaction.

The case of Miriam Weeks is not an outlier by any stretch of the imagination. Pornography is becoming darker and more violent than it has ever been. I first began to realize this when I began meeting girls, both at high schools and universities, who were telling me stories about the types of things guys were asking them to do, pushing them to do. It didn't seem to make a lot of sense to me, that bizarre sexual behavior would be considered the norm. I think of a few girls outside a Toronto high school, where we were discussing abortion and the case of rape. As they walked away, they called back, "You went to high school twenty years ago. You have no idea what guys are like now."

That's when I realized that this was probably a learned behavior.

Porn and sexual violence

I began contacting experts in the field, people who had studied the impact of pornography on men and women. The most revealing and chilling interview I conducted was with Dr. Mary Anne Layden, director of the Sexual Trauma and Psychopathology Program in the Department of Psychiatry at the University of Pennsylvania. I had cited her work on pornography and violence before, and wanted to see what sort of things her research had uncovered.

"Why," I asked Dr. Layden, "did you start researching the links between violence and pornography?"

"When I started as a psychotherapist, just about thirty years ago, I started treating patients who were victims of sexual violence and felt a special call to the damage that sexual violence did to these patients," she replied.

"When I had been doing the work for about ten years, because I'm a little bit of a slow learner, it occurred to me that I had not treated one case of sexual violence that didn't involve pornography... some were rape cases, some were incest cases, some were child molestation cases, some were sexual harassment cases—in all of these different kinds of cases, pornography showed up in every single one."

"So I said, there seems to be some connection here. Over time, I got interested in what is common in the perpetrators of sexual violence because I realized we were never going to solve the problem of sexual violence by treating victims who've been damaged by the problem and treating them one at a time and trying to put them back together. There weren't enough therapists in the world. There were too many victims in the world. We couldn't solve this by pulling them out of the river one at a time. We were going to have to go upstream and see who was pushing them in."

And as Dr. Layden discovered, it was the porn industry that was pushing people into the river. Men are not born rapists, she pointed out to me. But for some reason, many are increasingly justifying sexual violence. Why? Because pornography has turned the bodies of women and girls into a commodity. It is shaping the way men see women.

"It's a product," Dr. Layden said, her voice getting more emphatic.

> This is a business and I think that a lot of pimps would stop doing this if there wasn't any money involved, but it's a business and as soon as you tell somebody it's a product, as soon as you say this [is] something you buy, then this is something you can steal. Those two things are hooked. If you can buy it, you can steal it, and even better if you steal it because then you don't pay for it. So the sexual exploitation industry, whether it's strip clubs or prostitution or pornography, is where you buy it. Sexual violence is where you steal it – rape and child molestation and sexual harassment is where you steal it.
>
> So these things are all seamlessly connected. There isn't a way to draw a bright line of demarcation between rape and prostitution and pornography and child molestation. There are not bright lines of demarcation. The perpetrators are in a common set of beliefs, and when we look at the research we can see some of those common beliefs, so that we know that individuals who are exposed to pornographic media have beliefs such as [thinking that] rape victims like to be raped, they don't suffer so much when they're raped, 'she got what she wanted' when she was raped, women make false accusations of rape because it isn't really rape, sex is really either good or great and there isn't any other option other than good or great, no one is really traumatized by it.
>
> All of these are part of the rape myth. People who use pornography accept the rape myth to a greater degree than others. So we have a sense that pornography is teaching them to think like a rapist and then triggering them to act like rapists.

Pornography, like all other products, has done to the female body what economics always does to any product: If you commodify something, you cheapen it. It's really that simple.

But when your marketing strategy is inflaming lust and appealing to a hunger for power by degrading women, there are devastating results. As Dr. Layden pointed out to me, we even stop seeing each other as human.

"When you cheapen sex and you cheapen women's bodies, when you treat people like things, there's a consequence and one of the consequences is sexual violence but one of the consequences is also relationship damage," she pointed out.

> There's an interesting series of studies that actually highlights a bit of the phenomena of how this works. They were showing people just mildly sexualized pictures. They were men and women in swimsuits, men and women in their underwear, sort of relatively mild sexualized pictures and they showed them either upside right or upside down and looked at the processing in the brain, because it will display a phenomena of which part of your brain you're using to process that picture that you see.
>
> What we see with men, when people look at men, and look at them in their swimsuits or in their underwear, they're using the part of their brain that processes humans and human faces, but when we look at women in their swimsuits and their underwear we use the part of our brain that processes tools and objects. When you process a woman as a tool or an object you use. The rules that we use when we deal with tools or objects is if it's not doing its job then throw it away, get another one.
>
> So the feminists years ago said these men are treating women as sex objects and we thought that was a metaphor. It wasn't a metaphor. It was an actual statement of reality, that they're using the part of their brain which they use to process objects and things and there's a consequence in the society when you start treating sex as a product and women as a thing.

It was these first-hand experiences that launched Dr. Layden's research, which she highlights in a fascinating and disturbing paper called "Pornography and Violence: A New

Look at Research." Among other things, she definitively and emphatically connects sexual violence with pornography:

> For many reasons, as we shall see, pornography is a very effective teacher of beliefs and behaviors, and one that also teaches its users that the behaviors are acceptable and stimulates them to do so…
>
> Males who viewed sexual violence obtained higher scores both on scales measuring acceptance of interpersonal violence and the rape myth [the belief that women actually enjoy rape and suffer few negative consequences], when compare to males who viewed either a physically violent or neutral film. The increase in attitudes supporting sexual violence following exposure to pornography is greater if the pornography is violent than if it is non-violent.
>
> A similar effect is seen even when the pornography is not violent. Males who are shown non-violent scenes that sexually objectified and degraded women and were then exposed to material that depicted rape indicated that the rape victim experienced pleasure and 'got what she wanted.'
>
> Even women who were exposed to pornography as a child have a greater acceptance of the rape myth than those who were not. Those exposed to pornography recommend a sentence for a rapist that was half of that recommended by those who had been shown non-pornographic imagery. These subjects appear to have trivialized the crime of rape.[58]

Correlation and causation

Layden's research is confirmed elsewhere as well. The Berkmen Center for Internet and Society at Harvard Law School is one example:

> [Excerpts of the] Report of the Attorney General's Commission on Pornography:

> Section 5.2.1 Sexually Violent Material
>
> [C]linical and experimental research ... [has] focused particularly on sexually violent material, [and] the conclusions have been virtually unanimous. In both clinical and experimental settings, exposure to sexually violent materials has indicated an increase in the likelihood of aggression. More specifically, the research, ... shows a causal relationship between exposure to material of this type and aggressive behavior towards women.
>
> ...The evidence also strongly supports the conclusion that substantial exposure to violent sexually explicit material leads to a greater acceptance of the 'rape myth,' in its broader sense – that women enjoy being coerced into sexual activity, that they enjoy being physically hurt in sexual context, and that as a result a man who forces himself on a woman sexually is in fact merely acceding to the 'real' wishes of the woman, regardless of the extent to which she seems to be resisting...[59]

I make pains to belabor this point simply because over and over again, porn defenders, especially men, try to tell me that porn does not, in fact, fuel rape culture or trivialize sexual assault, with some actually claiming that men who would perhaps be rapists use pornography as a more "legitimate" outlet, thus saving someone a world of pain.

But the evidence simply doesn't bear that conclusion out. Covenant Eyes has taken great pains to compile research done into the correlation between pornography, sexual violence, and male attitudes towards sexual violence. Consistently, and without exception, the evidence proves correlation between porn and sexual assault:

> In a meta-analysis of 46 studies published from 1962 to 1995, comprising a total sample of 12,323 people, researchers concluded pornographic material puts one at increased risk of developing sexually deviant tendencies (31% increase in risk), committing sexual

> offenses (22% increase in risk), accepting rape myths (31% increase in risk).
>
> In a meta-analysis of 24 studies conducted between 1980 and 1993, with a total of 4,268 participants, researchers positively correlated rape myth acceptance to exposure to nonviolence or violent pornography.
>
> Among perpetrators of sex crimes, adolescent exposure to pornography is a significant predictor of elevated violence and victim humiliation.
>
> In a study of 187 female university students, researchers concluded early exposure to pornography was related to subsequent "rape fantasies" and attitudes supportive of sexual violence against women. Researchers believe pornography consumed at a young age contributes to women being socialized to accept sexual aggression as a sexual/romantic event.
>
> Japanese males were divided into three groups and each exposed to different types of home video pornography: a positive rape film (where the female expressed pleasure), a negative rape film (where the female expressed pain), or a consenting sex film. Those who viewed the positive rape film were significantly more likely to state that women could enjoy rape and [that] higher percentages of rape cases are invented by victims.
>
> In a study of 804 Italian adolescents, ages 14 to 19 years old, viewing pornography was correlated to both active and passive sexual violence and unwanted sex.[60]

Two things really stand out from these studies: The fact that pornography can socialize women and girls to accept sexual abuse, and the fact that pornography can turn people into predators.

50 Shades of Grey and the Normalization of Sexual Abuse

For anyone who has somehow managed to miss the gargantuan stacks of these books in every Walmart, airport, and bookstore,

50 Shades of Grey is an ongoing and explosive cultural phenomenon—a porn novel that evolved into a trilogy, which was then produced as a blockbuster Hollywood film. This phenomenon celebrates the seduction and manipulation of an insecure wallflower by a powerful businessman who likes to spend his recreational time engaging in a practice popularly referred to as BDSM—bondage, domination, sadism, and masochism.

I'm always a bit stunned that when condemning BDSM, I have to go any further than explaining the acronym: bondage, domination, sadism, and masochism. The fact that BDSM is an overt attack on human dignity should be obvious. That, unfortunately, is not the case—even with Christians. When media outlets announced that the book had sold over 100 million copies, I wrote a column to express my disgust:

> A lot of people seem to be taken with these books, especially based on the number of people I've seen unashamedly reading it at airports. These porn novels are "hot," many reviewers tell us confidently.
>
> Consider this, for just a moment: In a culture where broken families are often the norm, we have a generation of girls often growing up without fathers, never receiving the paternal love and affection that they need. Thus the famous "Daddy Issues" that so many comedy sitcoms repulsively mock, as if hurting girls seeking love and affection in all the wrong places is some sort of joke. Conversely, boys are also growing up without fathers, never having a positive male role model in the home to teach them how to treat women with love and respect. And what is teaching them how to treat girls? At an enormous rate, the answer is online pornography, which increasingly features violence against girls and women. The average first exposure of boys to pornography is age eleven. It is an absolutely toxic mess—insecure and hurting girls seek love from boys who have been taught how to treat them by the worst of pornography.
>
> Introduce into this situation a book, written by a woman,

> glorifying the idea that girls should expect or even enjoy pain and torture inside of a sexual relationship. How does a girl, insecure and unsure, know what to think? The culture around her now expects her not to need a safe relationship, but a "safe word" to employ in case her sadist partner gets a bit too carried away in the pain-making. Boys who might never have dreamed of asking a girl to subject herself to such pain and humiliation are now of course emboldened to request or even expect this fetishized sexual assault as a matter of course in a relationship. After all, much of pornography now features this degradation of girls and women, and a woman wrote a book celebrating such things. It might seem sadistic and rapey, but hey, sexual freedom has allowed us to celebrate "bondage" and sexual liberation has allowed us to liberate our darkest demons from the recesses of our skulls and allow them out to play in the bedroom. Boys used to get taught that they shouldn't hit girls, but now the culture is telling them that it's actually a turn-on.
>
> I genuinely feel sorry for many teenage girls trying to navigate the new, pornified dating landscape. I genuinely feel sorry for the legions of fatherless boys, exposed to pornography before they even had a chance to realize what it was, enfolded by the tentacles of perverted sexual material before they even realize what, exactly, they are trifling with. It brings to mind something C.S. Lewis once wrote: "Wouldn't it be dreadful if some day in our own world, at home, men start going wild inside, like the animals here, and still look like men, so that you'd never know which were which."[61]

The backlash to my thesis was immediate. What surprised me the most was the number of Christians who not only read this book, but were willing to defend this book loudly and explain why they thought it was appropriate to read. Regardless of the fact that the "heroine" of this story had been subjected to all kinds of sexual torture, many readers held up the flimsy idea of "consent" as a defence of *50 Shades of Grey*, rather than actually explaining how such behavior could be conducive to a loving relationship. In today's culture, it seems, even Christians place the value of orgasm above that of human dignity.

The idea of "consent" is a flimsy basis for justifying any and all sexual behavior (we should, I think, be appealing to a much higher authority than that in the first place) because not all consent is equal. Just because someone consents to something, that doesn't mean it's not abusive. If someone consents to being beaten up, punched, slapped, whipped, and called disgusting and degrading names, for example, does that make it any less reprehensible, or any less abusive?

Anyone who works with the victims of domestic and sexual assault will tell you that just because someone permits something to happen or doesn't extricate themselves from a situation doesn't mean it isn't, in fact, abuse. Activities that would have been seen as an assault on the dignity of the human person only a short time ago are now being normalized. Only when it comes to sex are people starting to defend such behavior, just so they can cling to their degrading fetishes and justify their turn-ons. Those women who defend the book because they think it spiced up their sex life are being incredibly selfish and negligent, refusing to acknowledge how this book will affect other women and girls in other situations.

Amy Bonomi, Lauren Altenburger, and Nicole Walton published an article on the impact of *50 Shades of Grey* in the *Journal of Women's Health*. Their conclusions are intuitive and horrifying:

> While intimate partner violence (IPV) affects 25% of women and impairs health, current societal conditions—including the normalization of abuse in popular culture such as novels, film, and music—create the context to support such violence.
>
> Emotional abuse is present in nearly every interaction, including: stalking (Christian deliberately follows Anastasia and appears in unusual places, uses a phone and computer to track Anastasia's whereabouts, and

> delivers expensive gifts); intimidation (Christian uses intimidating verbal and nonverbal behaviors, such as routinely commanding Anastasia to eat and threatening to punish her); and isolation (Christian limits Anastasia's social contact). Sexual violence is pervasive—including using alcohol to compromise Anastasia's consent, as well as intimidation (Christian initiates sexual encounters when genuinely angry, dismisses Anastasia's requests for boundaries, and threatens her). Anastasia experiences reactions typical of abused women, including: constant perceived threat ("my stomach churns from his threats"); altered identity (describes herself as a "pale, haunted ghost"); and stressful managing (engages in behaviors to "keep the peace," such as withholding information about her social whereabouts to avoid Christian's anger). Anastasia becomes disempowered and entrapped in the relationship as her behaviors become mechanized in response to Christian's abuse.
>
> Our analysis identified patterns in Fifty Shades that reflect pervasive intimate partner violence—one of the biggest problems of our time. Further, our analysis adds to a growing body of literature noting dangerous violence standards being perpetuated in popular culture.[62]

Indeed, many advocates for victims of domestic violence have come out against the *50 Shades of Grey* phenomenon. Clare Phillipson of Wearside Women in Need, which is a charity for victims, is nothing short of furious at the book's popularity, referring to it as a "manual for sexual torture."

"There will be a whole generation of young women hearing the women around them say: 'What a great book,' a generation of 13 and 14 year olds picking it up and thinking, 'This is all right,'' Phillipson noted. "We are saying, could people try reading it again and thinking: 'What is this man [Christian Grey] really about? It really is about a domestic violence perpetrator, taking someone who is less powerful, inexperienced, not entirely confident about the area of life she is being led into, and then spinning her a yarn. Then he starts doing absolutely horrific sexual things to her ... He gradually moves her boundaries, normalising the violence against her. It's the whole mythology that women want to be hurt."[63]

And that's because the dark world of "BDSM" and *50 Shades of Grey* is more about violence and control than it is about love or even sex. In fact, it is difficult for someone to give "consent" when they are restrained with various bondage gear. And sure enough, the far-left news site *Salon* published an exposé of rampant rape in the BDSM community some time ago. (Shocking, isn't it, that a community built around the celebration of violent sexual behaviors would be plagued by sexual violence?)

In fact, as the *Salon* article notes, one prominent sex activist, Kittie Stryker, noted that she has yet to meet a single female in the so-called "community" that "hasn't had some sort of sexual assault happen to her." The response of Stryker and others is to try and create a "Culture of Consent"—because yes, that's how bad it is. "Rape fantasies" are rapidly and increasingly turning into brutal rapes—because unfortunately for those who have a schizophrenic view of sexual violence, we do not have one brain for reality and one brain for fantasy.[64]

These sexual assaults, of course, are most often dutifully covered up.

The porn industry is working hard to make sure that you don't find out about such things. Every group seeking social acceptance hides their more distasteful elements when pushing for social acceptance, and the BDSM community is no different. They are attempting to sideline the most extreme manifestations of their commercialized sexual violence peddling in order to convince people that BDSM is just another harmless lifestyle.

Peter Acworth, the CEO of the huge BDSM porn company Kink, announced that it has stopped production of some of its more extreme sub-sites. These sites include public porn shoots in which the public is invited to spit on and verbally and physically abuse the female porn actresses. They're attempting a "rebrand," Acworth is telling media outlets. They want to be seen as mainstream.

Increasingly, they are mainstream. Mainstream enough, in fact, that celebrities charged with sexual assault are already using their affinity for BDSM to try stave off sexual assault charges, like former CBC radio host Jian Ghomeshi, who referred to his sexual proclivities as *50 Shades of Grey* when he was accused—and subsequently charged—with sexual assault. The media outlets reporting on the story accidentally said more than they intended to at the time. The sub-headline to the *Toronto Star's* breaking news story "CBC fires Jian Ghomeshi over sex allegations" is one such time: "Ousted host of Q denies claims by three women of unwanted sexual violence and threatens to sue…"[65]

Increasingly, people who have gotten on board with the torture porn and BDSM phenomenon are not even trying to deny that what they are engaging in, or watching, is sexual violence. As the *Toronto Star* put it, it is simply *unwanted* sexual violence.

Porn's violent ideology is spreading

My personal conversations with hundreds of high school students across the country have given me a heart-breaking glimpse of how this generation struggles with the virus of pornography that has infected their homes and their schools, their social networks and their entertainment. And thus, an article in the *Daily Telegraph* of the United Kingdom some time ago called "Pornography has changed the landscape of adolescence beyond all recognition" did not surprise me at all, in spite of the appalling details it revealed.

Columnist Allison Pearson was describing a recent conversation between herself and a number of other parents. "Porn has changed the landscape of adolescence beyond all recognition," she noted. "Like other parents of our generation, we were on a journey without maps or lights, although the instinct to protect our children from the darkness was overwhelming."

It was when a doctor in the group spoke up that the group was stunned into silence. According to Pearson:

> A GP, let's call her Sue, said: "I'm afraid things are much worse than people suspect." In recent years, Sue had treated growing numbers of teenage girls with internal injuries caused by frequent anal sex; not, as Sue found out, because she wanted to, or because she enjoyed it—on the contrary—but because a boy expected her to. "I'll spare you the gruesome details," said Sue, "but these girls are very young and slight and their bodies are simply not designed for that."
>
> Her patients were deeply ashamed at presenting with such injuries. They had lied to their mums about it and felt they couldn't confide in anyone else, which only added to their distress. When Sue questioned them further, they said they were humiliated by the experience, but they had simply not felt they could say no. Anal sex was standard among teenagers now, even though the girls knew that it hurt.[66]

And where are these brutal expectations coming from? Every adult knew without asking: pornography. Anal sex, especially violent anal sex, is now mainstream in porn, as the research of Dr. Gail Dines and others show us.

This is resulting in a sharp upswing in emotional problems among girls, something I've seen time and time again when interacting with high school students as well. Researchers with the *Journal of Adolescent Health,* Pearson reports, have been shocked to see a 7% spike in emotional issues in a mere five years—and in girls between the ages of 11 to 13. In a culture saturated with pornography, girls especially feel the pressure to conform to the fantasy that has consumed the minds of boys and spilled out to invade their reality.

All of these problems are interconnected. "Take female insecurity, warp and magnify it in the internet Hall of Mirrors, add a longing to be 'fit' and popular, then stir into a ubiquitous porn culture, and you have a hellish recipe for sad, abused girls," Pearson writes. "It explains why more than four in 10 girls between the ages of 13 and 17 in England say they have been coerced into sex acts, according to one of the largest

European polls on teenage sexual experience. Recent research by the Universities of Bristol and Central Lancashire found that a fifth of girls had suffered violence or intimidation from their teenage boyfriends, a high proportion of whom regularly viewed pornography, with one in five boys harbouring "extremely negative attitudes towards women."[67]

Up until now, the response has been a feeble attempt at further sex education, which many experts think may have a hand in the problem to begin with—once you permit and even encourage teen sex, it's very hard to unring that bell. And once those teenagers start taking their cues from an increasingly misogynist entertainment culture, a hypersexualized marketing industry, and violent pornography, you have all the ingredients you need to create a rape culture. The sex education being used now is not working, Pearson writes angrily—"not when tens of thousands of girls are revealing 'serious distress and harm following abusive behavior from boyfriends.'"

The result? That is what Pearson's doctor friend deals with, the medical treatment of young girls who got treated like porn stars—brutally abused and coerced into things they didn't want to do. "Young girls—children, really—who abase themselves to pass for normal in a grim, pornified culture," says Pearson. "Another study of British teenagers found that most youngsters' first experience of anal sex occurred within a relationship, but it was 'rarely under circumstances of mutual exploration of sexual pleasure.' Instead, it was the boys who pushed the girls to try it, with boys reporting that they felt 'expected' to take that role."[68]

In times past, porn theatres and smut shops were labeled "for adults only." But the sad reality now is that children, adolescents and teenagers are being forced to grow up in an adult world—and those adults have unleashed a tsunami of depravity unrivaled in human history for sheer accessibility. The Sexual Revolution is a revolution no longer, and all of its central tenets have been institutionalized by the authorities and educational system.

These stories are increasingly common, with news headlines such as "Porn drives youngsters to violence during sex," where a stunned journalist writes that, "Extreme pornography is driving thousands of young people to commit sex attacks, a study shows. Some nine percent of 14 to 21 year olds admitted to carrying out some sort of sexual violence, including 1 in 50 who had raped someone. Those perpetrators tended to report 'more frequently being exposed to media that depicted sexual and violent situation,' the poll of 1,058 people found."[69]

Pornography is turning kids into predators—and turning some boys into rapists without them even knowing they are. Porn, after all, is the new normal. How are adolescents to know that the sex they've grown up watching isn't real?

So why does any girl decide to be a porn star?

"If porn is as bad as you say it is, why does anyone still work in porn?"

This is a common response to anti-porn advocates who argue that pornography is sexually violent, the visual celebration of rape and a perverse glorification of the degradation of women and girls.

There are, of course, many answers to this question: Some women are desperate for money; many, if not most, have been sexually abused; still others have been deceived into thinking that the porn business is a glamorous and sexy business (the mainstreaming of Playboy and the increasing crossover of porn stars into other entertainment industries has certainly contributed to that).

But to find out what women experience inside the porn industry firsthand, I decided to call someone who'd been through it herself: Shelley Lubben.

Shelley Lubben was a porn star in the 1990s, having entered the industry as a prostitute at a very young age. The "sexual exploitation industries," as Dr. Mary Anne Layden refers to the various aspects of the sex business, soon began to take their toll.

"It's a vicious circle [being] a sex worker, because you're stripping, taxi dancing, and you just get burned out in prostitution," Lubben told me. "After prostitution I got burned out, and I was lied to that I would be safe from STDs (sexually transmitted diseases) and I would make all this money. I was a single parent, so what the heck, might as well do sex on camera. But it was completely and utterly the worst, darkest thing I've ever been involved in."

For starters, Lubben had assumed that unlike in prostitution, where many of the johns didn't want to use condoms, the porn industry would at least keep her safe from STDs. It didn't—and that's because, as Lubben tells it, the entire porn industry is rife with them.

"We didn't use condoms in porn," she said bluntly. "There's no condoms allowed, so we're forced to do unprotected sex—and I can't tell you how many people alter their tests. Just last year, they had 4 HIV cases, a high bunch out of a very small group of people...we know that most of the porn stars have had an STD at one time or another, and they estimate between 66% to 99% have herpes. They don't test for herpes, so all these people are involved with rampant STDs."

> Even the LA Public Health Department shows they've been monitoring and they came up with thousands and thousands [of cases] of chlamydia and gonorrhea. They're the highest group in California to have that many STDs. So when people click [on porn], they're contributing to sex trafficking, they're contributing to STDs, they're contributing to people who are mostly alcohol to drug addicts. Now I'm speaking of the majority. Not every porn star's a drug addict, but the majority of them are. And I can't tell you, when I went through recovery, I had PTSD. I had all kinds of disorders, serious traumas.

It's a story I have read time and time again in my research on the porn industry, so I had to ask: why did she get involved in the sexual exploitation industries in the first place?

"Well, I'd been sexually abused at nine years old by a teenage boy and his sister," Shelley Lubben replied. "So I experienced very shocking heterosexual and homosexual activity at a very young age, and at the same time I was raised by the television - I was allowed to watch R-rated movies, horror movies, movies with sexual content, so I learned about love and sex from abuse and from basically parental neglect, because they would just allow us to watch these things.

> And then as I got older, I was rebelling because my dad was not very involved in my life, and I began to look for sex with boys because the boys would say they loved me. So it was this cycle that I felt in my head that I'm loved if I have sex with a person. My dad kicked me out on the street for being rebellious, and I ended up in San Fernando, LA, which is Porn Valley, and a pimp lured me in, and I was very naïve. No, I was *rebellious,* I was not naïve. He lured me in for 35 dollars, and then he... you know, I had to escape from him physically, because he became very abusive, and then a Madame found me, and it just spiraled on.

Once she was embedded, Lubben felt trapped in a cycle of degradation and destruction.

"I would hate prostitution, feel guilty, then I would do stripping to survive," she said. "I had no education—most of these girls that enter porn do not really have an education, there's gonna be maybe a few that say they have degrees, although I have yet to see one—but most of the girls don't come from, like, healthy families, where they have a healthy self-esteem. I haven't really met porn stars with really healthy families. That doesn't mean they don't exist, but maybe they exist in their mind because of course different girls are gonna wanna say they're empowered by their sex work, because what you can't beat, you're gonna join. You don't want people to think you're weak when you're in porn; you wanna act like you love it and you love rough stuff, and you love being violated, and called degrading names. It's all just a pack of lies. People do porn because they need the money, and most of them don't have other options or education."

The porn industry is dark, evil, and incredibly violent—and it has been that way for a very long time. I read Lubben some of

Dr. Gail Dines' research on how pornography is becoming more violent, and then asked her if that reflected her experience.*

"Absolutely," she replied. "It was even violent back in my day, but I got involved in hard-core porn just because I was still filled with rage from my parents. But yeah, in my day I would have never let anyone rip my mouth or put some weird gadget in my mouth or do something where they're causing a rectum prolapse, I wouldn't have done that. I would've walked away. Nowadays, girls have to end up doing that stuff, 'cause that's what sells. So it's really sad this is a lot of our society that, but you know, everyone's so desensitized to vanilla sex now. They want it harder, and grosser and darker, and you know, I can't imagine what our society will be like in 20 years from now. I can't, I don't think I… I'll have to like move to the mountains or something, because I doubt any normal girl could walk the street at that point."

It's shocking in some ways that the porn industry is so mainstream and so popular, considering that at the same time there had been a chorus of voices speaking out against sex trafficking. Doesn't the porn industry, I asked Lubben, feed into sex trafficking?

"A lot of people think that pornography fuels sex trafficking and it does," Lubben said firmly. "But it does that because it *is* sex trafficking. It's called [a] cutthroat business because it's trafficking; all of us have been coerced into doing a scene we didn't wanna do. We went to fraudulent doctors or fraudulent clinics they sent us to. In fact, their clinics—the main porn star clinic closed down a couple years ago, because a lot of us were standing against it—but we had a former porn actress who has a PhD in sexology, and she would put on a white lab coat and tell the girls, 'Call me Dr. Sharon Mitchell.' So all these girls think that she's a medical doctor, and they would go there for her medical advice and for STD treatment and testing. So that's just one way they're fraudulent."

* Dr. Gail Dines' book *Pornland: How Porn Has Hijacked Our Sexuality* is one of the most mauling things I have ever read. In this chapter and the preceding one, I have tried to condense an enormous amount of information while leaving out much of the explicit and graphic descriptions Dines utilizes in her work. As valuable as her research is, I don't recommend that a casual reader pick up *Pornland*. One of my intentions in providing this research was to allow others to gain a full picture of the brutality of the porn industry without having to expose themselves to the raw material.

> Another way [is that] pornographers make false promises: 'If you do this scene I promise that you're going to get this money, or you're going to get the box cover' or, 'You won't have to do this kind of scene anymore.' It's all based on lies. And so you've gotta be tough to be in that business.
>
> You know, most of these films are made in private locations, and private mansions, or hotel rooms where's there's no government access. So it's like two young girls, 18, 19, 20-year-old girls on a mostly older male set. The producer's male, the crew's male…so of course, we're intimidated into doing scenes we don't wanna do. I can't tell you how many times I've showed up and they said, 'You need to do this scene,' [and] I said, 'No, that's not what my agent said,' or 'That's not what I was told to do,' and they're like, 'Well, you're gonna do it or we're not gonna pay you, we're going to sue you.' And now with the Internet they tell the girls, 'If you don't do this scene, we're going to send your porn to your family members, we're gonna ruin your reputation, you're never gonna work again, we're gonna take away your finances, we're gonna physically hurt you,' or they threaten to sue them. This is sex trafficking. Every porn star has been trafficked at least at one time or another in the porn industry.

It is because of this that Shelley Lubben, after eight years, finally left the porn industry after meeting a pastor, who later married her, sticking with her through ten long, painful years of recovery. In 2007, she started the Pink Cross Foundation, which works to bring porn actresses and porn actors out of the porn industry, offering them hope and healing. They work to warn young people enamored with the industry of the darkness and pain that awaits them within.

Before I hung up the phone, I asked Shelley Lubben one final question: "If you could say one thing to someone who's looking at pornography, what would you say?"

She barely had to pause. "You're contributing to your demise," she answered. "And to your family's demise, and your wife's.

I can't tell you how many porn addicts have lost their families and jobs. It's really sad. And they're contributing to children being raped. I'm like—for a better reason not to click on porn, [think about] child porn. Just think, right now as I've been talking to you, there are little children that are being drugged and raped. How could anyone click on porn knowing that?"[70]

A compelling question. If porn users actually researched the impact of pornography on those who "star" in it, I suspect there would be far fewer porn users. One former porn producer told me that the girls he recruited to star in porn shoots showed up bright-eyed, looking forward to fame and fortune. Then, the porn industry worked its grotesque transformation. "I literally watched their souls die," he said quietly.

Or as Tanya Burleson, known in the porn world as Jersey Jaxin, describes it: "Guys are punching you in the face. You get ripped. Your insides can come out of you. It's never ending. You're viewed as an object — not as a human with a spirit. People do drugs because they can't deal with the way they're being treated."

Sexual cannibalism

When guys have been looking at porn for a long time, it's a tough habit to break. And when you're an anti-porn speaker, it's tough to figure out how to make people quit a habit that has deeply rewired their brain and reshaped their attractions, *using just words*. So one of the things I've tried to do is illustrate just how evil porn is, by calling it what it is.

Porn is, at its root, sexual cannibalism.

Think about it. Sex is supposed to be two people unashamedly giving themselves to one another in love. Sex is supposed to be all about the other person. That's why, before our vocabulary started becoming far cruder and more truncated, we used to call it "making love." But watching pornography is the precise opposite of giving.

Pornography is someone sexually consuming another for one-sided pleasure. That person exists only to fulfill his pleasures, his fantasies, his satisfaction. Sexual cannibalism.

There is something grotesquely cannibalistic about men arousing themselves to the physical destruction of the feminine on screen. There is something carnivorous about men watching women get violated and degraded for recreation and entertainment.

After all, carnality, cannibalism, carnivore, and carnage all have the same root word: Carnae, or flesh. Our carnality, fleshly lust, is leading directly into sexual cannibalism—and the carnage of the porn industry manifests itself in destructive or destroyed relationships, shattered marriages, twisted minds, and broken porn stars.

Those broken porn stars, of course, are simply collateral damage. They join the industry, often with high hopes, and leave angry and cynical, if not irreparably diseased and suffering from PTSD. But the sex-driven mob bays for more young girls, more flesh to consume and discard. Do we even think, I often wonder, about the humans in the pornography we watch? Does anyone ever wonder how they got there? Why they stay there? How it impacts them?

Rarely, of course. Because if we did, we'd stop watching. Sexual cannibalism is our culture's addiction to the flesh of others. But as we know, cannibalism isn't healthy.

We just need to realize that engaging pornography is essentially playing Russian roulette. As philosopher Roger Scruton sombrely noted, "Those who become addicted to this 'risk-free' form of sex run a risk of another and greater kind. They risk the loss of love, in a world where only love brings happiness."

And now we have created, within the space of a generation, a society that can in many ways legitimately be called a "rape culture." Millions upon millions of men are addicted to the destruction of women, and increasingly, they are seeking to act out their dark fantasies in real life. Desire has turned to lust, lust has turn to misogyny, and a perpetual diet of porn has mutated this misogyny into something worse. So yes, "rape culture" exists. But it is not what many of the feminists and secularists say it is. It's time we started paying attention to the rape culture growing right before our eyes.

Chapter 5

The Human Cost of the Culture Wars

The toughest part of a D&E abortion is extracting the baby's head. The head of a baby that age is about the size of a large plum and is now free floating inside the uterine cavity. You can be pretty sure you have hold of it if the Sopher clamp is spread about as far as your fingers will allow. You will know you have it right when you crush down on the clamp and see white gelatinous material coming through the cervix. That was the baby's brains. You can then extract the skull pieces. Many times a little face will come out and stare back at you.

—Dr. Anthony Levatino, former abortionist

Every revolution has its victims, those human beings who are sacrificed on the altar of the new reigning ideology. The Sexual Revolution was no different. It is portrayed in popular culture and in university history classes as a joyous release of sexual energy that provided a catalyst for societal happiness—make love, not war. But bloody war was made, nonetheless. One of the greatest lies about the Sexual Revolution is that it was a bloodless revolution when, in fact, it has spawned the greatest carnage the world has ever seen. Our society doesn't use guillotines. But we kill voraciously, ruthlessly and incessantly. Millions upon millions of human beings developing in the womb are snuffed out each year in the most grotesque fashion.

In many ways, the push for legal abortion was an inevitable result of the Sexual Revolution. In the minds of millions, contraception and hook-up culture established that sex and reproduction were separate, if not unrelated. The staggering rise of sex outside of marriage ensured that suddenly, thousands of pregnancies were happening in less than ideal circumstances. And then, people began to realize that contraception was not quite as reliable as they'd been told. It turned out that one of the most natural human processes—reproduction—was harder to foil than everyone thought, and pills and paper-thin pieces of latex didn't always do the trick. It was easy for a birth control pill routine to be screwed up or skipped. Condoms broke. And of course, babies happened.

Preventative measures sometimes failed, and so for the Sexual Revolutionaries there could be only one solution: extermination. Or, as it has become known, abortion: the violent destruction of a human life developing within the womb of his or her mother. Societies based on Judeo-Christian principles had long recognized abortion as murder, and had prosecuted those who performed abortions as murderers. But with the rise of the Sexual Revolution, the times had changed. The old order had been discarded. New children would be too.

I remember the first time I came face to face with one of these murdered children. It was several years ago, at a conference of anti-abortion activists in California. I gave a speech on the history of social reform, on how those exposing the reality of abortion were following in the footsteps of the abolitionists, the National Child Labor Committee, and so many other activists who had fought to bring evidence of what was being inflicted on victims before the eyes of the public.

Later that weekend, one pro-life veteran pulled me aside and said he had something to show me. Something someone as young as me in the pro-life movement needed to see. I agreed, and we drove to his house in his truck. We pulled up at a detached garage and went inside.

He'd been through a dumpster behind an abortion clinic, he told me. That itself didn't surprise me—the practice has been common in the American pro-life movement for decades. Anti-abortion crusaders Joe Scheidler and Monica Miller* recovered battered, abandoned children from the trash to bury them, and

* *Abandoned: The Untold Story of the Abortion Wars* by Monica Miller describes these retrievals in heartbreaking detail.

photographs of their corpses were some of the first abortion victim photos the movement put to use to expose the killing. Activists like Lynn Mills* and Troy Newman** have utilized dumpster diving to collect evidence of wrongdoing on the part of the abortion industry. When children become trash, Christians become trash-collectors.

But for some reason, I still didn't expect the obvious. It's one thing to see photos of abortion victims, or even horrifying videos—I've seen enough footage of abortion procedures to last several lifetimes. It's an entirely different thing to look at a child in a jar. There's something about it that doesn't register—your eyes take in the sight, but your brain doesn't quite understand what it's looking at. After all, who has any mental context for a baby in a jar?

Yet that is what I was looking at. A jar on the table, with a little boy in it.

The baby boy was perfect, so perfect. His skin was ivory white, but everything else looked so normal. His eyes were closed, and his expression was serene and peaceful. Just holding the jar felt strange, because the little boy would move about in the liquid, his arms and legs sort of waving morbidly. I almost expected him to wake up. The only sign that all was not well were two little puncture wounds in the back of his skull, where the abortionist had killed him. I wondered how old he would be if he was alive. But he wasn't. He was frozen in time. Trapped in formaldehyde, he was floating in a jar on the table, and I couldn't take my eyes off of him.

My stomach still twists, just thinking back. Babies in jars. Babies in dumpsters. Babies in incinerators. That's our society now.

The culture war is not some abstract philosophical duel fought by politicians seeking to carve up voting blocs. The culture war is a real war, with real bodies. I know. I held one.

---

* Lynn Mills is a Michigan activist whose undercover work resulted in the prosecution of Dr. Jack Kevorkian, aka "Dr. Death."

** Troy Newman describes these tactics in his book *Abortion Free: Your Manual For Building A Pro-Life America One Community At A Time*, which he co-authored with Cheryl Sullenger.

Holding that baby reminded me of something Peter Hitchens once said to me. "I think that abortion is much beloved by revolutionaries," he noted darkly, "because they always like the mob to get their hands in blood and commit some sort of crime of their own." Shared guilt is a tremendously powerful force.

The first time around

It is important for people to understand that a society in which abortion is common and infanticide is on the rise is not something new. A pro-life movement rising up in response to these evils is not new, either. While many people labor under the misconception that the pro-life movement emerged quite suddenly after Canada decriminalized abortion in 1969 or when the US Supreme Court overturned the nation's abortion laws with *Roe v. Wade* in 1973, nothing could be further from the truth.

I am not writing here of the large and committed pro-life movement that existed, especially in the United States, decades prior to the advent of legal abortion. Dr. Daniel K. Williams of the University of West Georgia published a tremendous work of historical research in 2016, *Defenders of the Unborn: The Pro-Life Movement Before Roe v. Wade,* and even the *New York Times* review of the book was forced to admit that clearly, medical practitioners and activists had opposed abortion on human rights grounds long before the Supreme Court imposed legal abortion on all fifty states. What I am referring to is the fact that practices like abortion and infanticide have been accepted in the West at least twice within the last two thousand years. What the pro-life movement at the beginning of the twenty-first century faces, George Grant writes brilliantly in his book *Third Time Around: A History of the Pro-Life Movement from the First Century to the Present,* is the same evil that is now rearing its ugly head for the third time since the Crucifixion.

"Virtually every culture in antiquity was stained with the blood of innocent children," Grant explained.

> Unwanted infants in ancient Rome were abandoned outside the city walls to die from exposure to the elements or from the attacks of wild foraging beasts.

> Greeks often gave their pregnant women harsh doses of herbal or medicinal abortifacients. Persians developed highly sophisticated surgical curette procedures. Chinese women tied heavy ropes around their waists so excruciatingly tight that they either aborted or passed into unconsciousness. Ancient Hindus and Arabs concocted chemical pessaries—abortifacients that were pushed or pumped directly into the womb through the birth canal. Primitive Canaanites threw their children onto great flaming pyres as a sacrifice to their god Molech. Polynesians subjected their pregnant women to onerous tortures—their abdomens beaten with large stones or hot coals heaped upon their bodies. Japanese women straddled boiling cauldrons of parricidal brews. Egyptians disposed of their unwanted children by disemboweling and dismembering them shortly after birth—their collagen was then ritually harvested for the manufacture of cosmetic creams.[71]

It was the early church that first recognized that abortion and infanticide were wicked, cruel practices that destroyed children created in the image of God. Christian thinkers of the Apostolic Era condemned these practices unanimously and in the harshest of terms, from the bishop Ambrose to the apologist Tertullian to the titan Augustine of Hippo. Basil of Caesarea crusaded against a guild of abortionists he discovered in Caesarea, preaching incessantly against abortion and infanticide and going so far as to physically tear down an infanticide shrine. In 374 AD, Emperor Valentinian responded to Basil's war on the abortion industry by issuing a decree: "All parents must support their children conceived; those who brutalize or abandon them should be subject to the full penalty prescribed by law."[72] This was, Grant notes, "the first time in human history abortion, infanticide, exposure, and abandonment were made illegitimate."

It was not only Basil of Caesarea, either. Thousands of Christians responded to the wickedness they found in society by doing everything in their power to help the weakest and most vulnerable members of their society: Addai of Edessa, Benignus of Dijon, Callistus of Rome, Alban of Verlamium, Afra of Augsburg, George of Diospolis, Barlaam of Antioch—the list goes on. As Grant writes:

> The pro-life position of the early church was not mere dogma. The patristics matched their rhetoric with reality. They worked hard and sacrificed dearly for the sake of life. In Rome, Christians rescued babies that had been abandoned on the exposure walls outside the city—often illegally and at great risk to themselves. These foundlings would then be adopted and raised up in the nurture and admonition of the Lord.
>
> In Corinth, Christians offered charity, mercy, and refuge to temple prostitutes who had become pregnant—again, standing against the tide of community expectations. Those despised and exploited women were taken into homes where they could safely have their children and then get a fresh start on life.
>
> In Poitiers, Christians cared for the poor, the sick, and the lame in clinics and hostels. The church sacrificed its own personal peace and affluence by protecting and providing for those unwanted and dispossessed souls without partiality.
>
> Clearly, Christians were not simply against child-killing. They were for life. Whenever and wherever the gospel went out, believers emphasized the priority of good works, especially works of compassion toward the needy. For the first time in human history, hospitals were founded, orphanages were established, rescue missions were started, almshouses were built, soup kitchens were begun, shelters were endowed, charitable societies were incorporated, and relief agencies were commissioned. The hungry were fed; the naked, clothed; the homeless, sheltered; the sick, nursed; the aged, honored; the unborn, protected; and the handicapped, cherished.[73]

Across the Western world and beyond, the early Christians introduced concepts that were at that point fundamentally foreign. Child-killing practices were so common that even the fable of the founding of Rome spoke of two children—Romulus and Remus—being left to die. Now, they were suddenly and firmly rejected and opposed. The early Christian church did more than just engage in discussion on child-killing. They engaged the culture, and transformed it. For centuries, and on into the Middle Ages, Christians fought back the Culture of Death wherever it arose, refusing to allow it to take root and combatting it wherever it did.

The second time around

Then came the Renaissance, described by most historians as the era that bridged the medieval period and the modern era. Stretching from the fourteenth century to seventeenth century, people instinctively think of this period as an era filled with beautiful art, wonderful music, and great leaps forward in the fields of science and technology. This, of course, is true. But the Renaissance was not only a great leap forward. It was also, in many ways, a great leap backwards. The ruling classes, George Grant notes, were fascinated with the pagan past of the West. Augustine and Ambrose were ignored in favor of Aristotle and Plato. With a return to pagan philosophers came a return to pagan ideas:

> [The ruling classes] began to extol their pre-Christian values as well, including the values of abortion, infanticide, abandonment, and exposure. A complete reversion took place. Virtually all the great advances that the medieval era brought were lost in just a few short decades. By the middle of the epoch, as many as one out of every three children was killed or exposed in French, Italian, and Spanish cities. In Toulouse, the rate of known abandonment as a percentage of the number of recorded births varied from an approximate mean of 10 percent at the beginning of the era to a mean of about 17 percent at its end—with the final decades consistently above 20 and often passing 25 percent for the whole population of the city. In the poorer quarters of the city, the rate may have reached as high as 40 percent. In Lyons before the French Revolution, the number of

> cast-off, unwanted infants was approximately one-third the number of births. During the same period in Paris, children known to have been abandoned accounted for between 20 and 30 percent of all registered births. In Florence the rate ranged from a low of 14 percent of all babies to a high of just under 45 percent. In Milan, the opening of the age witnessed a rate of 16 percent. By its closing the percentage had actually risen to about 25 percent. In Madrid, the figures ranged anywhere from 14 to 26 percent, while in London, they were between 11 and 22 percent. Fragmentary evidence suggests comparable rates throughout the rest of Europe, wherever resurrected paganism was extolled.[74]

And again, for the second time since the Crucifixion, Christians rose up to combat brutal ideologies with love and compassion. Again, they did not merely advocate a theological belief, they engaged in life-saving action. Andrew Geddes, converted under the preaching of Scottish Reformer John Knox, sought to find and help abandoned children. Nicholas Ferrar, an English Puritan, left a London political career in 1625 to, among other things, help orphan boys with nowhere to go. Their names are many, and the lives they saved countless: Thomas of Villaneuva, Louise De Marillac, Otto Blumhardt, and John Eudes, to say nothing of titans like William Wilberforce, Thomas Clarkson, and Granville Sharp.*

It is very important to take note of something here: those who value the lives of pre-born children *have always valued the lives of all*. Abortion advocates love to tell lazy lies about the pro-life movement—*they only care about human life before birth, not after!* they like to say. But this has never been true. Christians started orphanages, shut down abortion rings, fought against slavery, abolished infanticide, and began crisis pregnancy centres. Wherever human beings created in God's image were threatened, it was the churches, first, who responded

* William Wilberforce, Thomas Clarkson, Granville Sharp, and a legion of others made up the abolitionist movement that successfully banned the slave trade in Great Britain. Eric Metaxas describes this campaign in vivid detail in his book *Amazing Grace: William Wilberforce and the Heroic Campaign to End Slavery.*

with compassion and assistance. As the preacher Charles Haddon Spurgeon once thundered, "The God that answers by orphanages, let Him be Lord!"

The third time around

The same is true for today's pro-life movement. As much as abortion advocates would like to claim that those fighting to expose the abortion industry and assist women in crisis only care about children in the womb, the evidence shows that nothing could be further from the truth. In the United States alone, there are more than 2,300 pregnancy resource centres serving nearly two million women every single year. Many of them, says The Witherspoon Institute, "stay at one of the 350 residential facilities for women and children operated by pro-life groups. In New York City alone, there are twenty-two centers serving 12,000 women a year. These centers provide services including pre-natal care, STI testing, STI treatment, ultrasound, childbirth classes, labor coaching, midwife services, lactation consultation, nutrition consulting, social work, abstinence education, parenting classes, material assistance, and post-abortion counseling."[75]

This is to say nothing of the enormous amount of charity work and financial assistance provided by churches and religious groups, which dwarf the contributions of those groups dedicated to legal abortion. The historical commitment of Christian organizations to the welfare and dignity of all human beings continues.

This time around, as I laid out in the preceding chapters, Christians in the West face a culture war with many fronts. Like a dragon with a dozen snarling heads, the decline of religious faith*, the Sexual Revolution, the contraceptive mentality, and the porn plague have created a monster that threatens to tear to shreds the moral fabric of our civilization. Hook-up culture creates a market for abortionists. The contraceptive mentality ensures that men and women do not see children as a gift, but an

---

* The impact of Charles Darwin's theory of natural selection will be dealt with in Chapter 6.

unwanted consequence of sex. Pornography further entrenches the view that sex does not result in children, but dehumanizes women as sex objects rather than recognizing them as wives and mothers, friends and colleagues. The cultural currents have created a perfectly deadly whirlpool, and in Canada and the United States, millions of pre-born children are tossed into the void every year. In Canada, nearly 300 children in the womb are violently decapitated, dismembered, and disemboweled each day. In the United States, that number approaches 3,000.

Science versus abortion

From nearly the very beginning of its existence as a new country, Canada respected all human life. Two years after Confederation, in 1869, abortion was made illegal. Abortionists could face up to life in prison. Similar laws were being installed across the United States of America.

A consensus was emerging across North America around this time, mainly pushed by Protestant doctors, that the science which had informed the field of medicine for some time was erroneous. The idea that "quickening"—the point at which the mother could feel the baby moving in her womb—was the point at which a baby was verifiably present was, it turned out, verifiably faulty science. Abortion laws were not laws left over from the Dark Ages, as abortion activists would claim later on. Rather, they were policies based on the newest scientific research. According to Daniel K. Williams in *Defenders of the Unborn*:

> Prior to the early nineteenth century, a number of Protestant doctors convinced state legislatures that medical science proved that biological life began long before quickening, which meant, in their view, that abortion should be prohibited at any state of fetal development. By the end of the nineteenth century, legislatures in nearly every state had enacted laws that allowed abortion only in cases in which the procedure was required to save a woman's life...The physicians behind this effort also embarked on an education campaign to convince the public of the value of fetal life. Armed with cases of glass slides showing the fetus at various stages of development, they traveled to

> libraries and civic groups across the country to spread the message that human development proceeds along a continuum, that quickening is a biologically meaningless stage, and that the embryo deserved protection from the moment of conception.[76]

Equipped with the scientific evidence that abortion ends the life of a human being developing in the womb, and dedicated to educating the public on this, the doctors who pushed for abortion bans found themselves wholeheartedly supported by the Roman Catholic Church as well as many Protestant churches and Christian organizations. A new social consensus emerged in a few short decades, based on a series of very simple premises: Killing human beings was wrong. Science revealed, quite definitively, that a human being was developing in the womb of the mother. Thus, abortion was an act of violence that ended the life of a human being, and should not be tolerated within a civilized society.

And for nearly 100 years, children in the womb were protected by law.

Legal abortion in Canada*

In 1969, exactly one century after Canada made the science-driven decision to make abortion illegal, Parliament passed Prime Minister Pierre Trudeau's Omnibus Bill. It was a gargantuan piece of legislation addressing dozens of different issues, liberalizing the law on everything from illegal sex acts, to contraception, and divorce. Abortion was technically still a criminal offence according to Section 251 of Canada's Criminal Code, but the door was opened far enough to ensure that many women could begin legally obtaining abortions.

Hospitals were permitted to set up Therapeutic Abortion Committees, each consisting of three doctors who would

---

* *Winning Choice on Abortion* by Ann Thomson, *Morgentaler: A Difficult Hero* by Catherine Dunphy, and *Ten Thousand Roses: The Making of a Feminist Revolution* by Judy Rebick are three first-hand accounts by abortion activists detailing the extensive campaigns to legalize abortion in Canada.

approve or disallow a woman's request for an abortion based on whether or not they judged the pregnancy to be a danger to her health or her life. The term "health" was left an intentionally ambiguous category, ensuring that doctors who supported abortion could approve abortion requests on the grounds that the woman's distress at not being permitted to have an abortion could negatively impact her health. A dichotomy soon sprung up within Canada's healthcare system: hospitals dominated by pro-life medical professionals refused all or nearly all abortion requests, and hospitals staffed mainly by medical professionals who supported abortion rubber-stamped nearly all of them. The abortion rate skyrocketed. Soon, "abortion was the second most common surgery after tonsillectomies."[77]

While pro-lifers decried the loss of life, abortion activists demanded that the remaining restrictions on abortion be removed. "Abortion on demand," they shrieked at rallies across the country, "and without apology!" The very same year Canada began permitting abortions, 1969, their hero emerged. Henry Morgentaler was a doctor and a Holocaust survivor, a man who believed that killing the unthinking fetuses in the wombs of distressed mothers would alleviate their distress and bring more happiness into the world. He was a utilitarian, and he was also an activist. He began performing abortions at his office in Quebec. In June of the following year, he was arrested for the first time.

While the fledgling pro-life movement fought desperately to gain political traction and install legal protections for pre-born children once again, abortion activists took to the streets. In 1970, the Vancouver Women's Caucus left Vancouver in a cavalcade of vehicles they called the Abortion Caravan, stopping at cities across Canada to stage demonstrations and create bizarre re-enactments of back alley abortions in what they called "guerilla theatre." Women joined them along the way, and they were welcomed by supposedly religious groups such as the United Church of Canada, which was already emerging as one of Henry Morgentaler's most devout backers. Upon arrival in Ottawa, thirty of the abortion activists chained themselves to railings inside the House of Commons, shutting down Parliament for the first time in Canadian history. People were listening.

Dr. Henry Morgentaler continued to commit illegal abortions and continued to get arrested for doing so. The justice system soon found itself in an uncomfortable position: a brazen and unrepentant criminal was flagrantly breaking the law, but no jury would convict him. The Quebec Court of Appeals actually had to overturn a jury acquittal in 1974, an unprecedented action upheld by the Canadian Supreme Court the following year. Even while serving an eighteen-month jail sentence, Morgentaler was acquitted by a jury on secondary charges. This time, the Quebec Court of Appeals let it stand.

Between 1969 and 1988, Morgentaler and his allies set up illegal abortion clinics, performed illegal abortions, and defiantly went to prison when they were raided by the police. Almost every time, juries acquitted the abortionists, and in 1988, Canada's Supreme Court tossed out all abortion restrictions in *R v. Morgentaler*, calling on Parliament to redraft abortion laws.

Canada's Parliament attempted to do so in 1990, and Bill C-43, which would have prohibited abortion except in cases where the mother's health was threatened was passed by Members of Parliament. The bill, however, failed on a tie vote in the Senate. With that failure, Canada achieved a status that only North Korea and China also hold: abortion legal throughout all nine months of pregnancy, for any reason, or for no reason at all.

To date, more than four million children developing in the womb have been killed by legal abortion in Canada.

Legal abortion in America

In the US, abortion activists started demanding the right to legally terminate the lives of pre-born children as well. In 1959, the American Law Institute proposed legalizing abortion in nearly half a dozen circumstances, including fetal deformity. On April 25, 1967, the ironically-named Governor John Love of Colorado followed their suggestion, legalizing abortion in cases of sexual assault as well as mental or physical disability of either the child in the womb or the mother. Such laws were intended to be ambiguous, so as to allow the maximum number of abortions possible. South Carolina, California, and Oregon soon followed suit.

Laws permitting abortion begin to pass in rapid succession. Governor Nelson Rockefeller of New York passed a law in 1970 permitting abortion on demand up until the 24th week of pregnancy, repealing a law that had been passed to protect children in the womb 140 years before. Washington, Hawaii, and Alaska passed similarly permissive laws. Two years later, thirteen states permitted abortion in some circumstances and four states actually allowed abortion on demand. Pro-lifers, many of them medical professionals, mobilized to halt the abortion movement's successes. In spite of setbacks, in 1972 thirty-one states still banned abortion in all instances with the exception of saving the mother's life, and Governor Nelson Rockefeller was actually forced to veto a repeal of New York's 1970 abortion-on-demand law. The pro-life movement was adapting to the situation, and doing so successfully.

On January 22, 1973, everything changed. In a decision that stunned the nation, the US Supreme Court issued its *Roe v. Wade* ruling.* Seven of the nine Supreme Court justices ruled that the constitutional right to privacy included a right to abortion. Further to that, they ignored the fact that abortion laws had initially been passed in the United States based on medical evidence that proved the humanity of the pre-born child, stipulating that no state could restrict abortion in the first trimester. In the second trimester, regulations could only be put in place to protect the health of the mother. In a ruling issued on the same day, the Court defined "health" in *Doe v. Bolton* to encompass a wide range of factors, including "physical, emotional, psychological, familial, and women's age."[78]

In one fell swoop, seven unelected judges threw out decades of established jurisprudence on the protection of life in the womb and ignored completely the scientific evidence that had in many cases led to such legislation in the first place. The pro-life movement's campaign to prevent legal abortion in the United States was reduced to shambles, as the laws of dozens of states were eradicated from the books and laws protecting the smallest and most vulnerable human beings were rendered

---

* The definitive history of this ruling was written by Clarke D. Forsythe in his 2013 book *Abuse of Discretion: The Inside Story of Roe v. Wade*.

illegal. Abortion clinics sprung up across the country, and open warfare on babies in the womb commenced in earnest.

To date, more than fifty million children developing in the womb have been killed by legal abortion in the United States.

LIES AND PROPAGANDA

"Political language," George Orwell once wrote, "is designed to make lies sound truthful and murder respectable, and to give an appearance of solidity to pure wind." There is perhaps no situation in which those words are more applicable than the rise of the "pro-choice" worldview in North America. It is one based on ignorance, ideology, the repudiation of scientific evidence, and outright deceit.

It is not my intention here to summarize the many pro-life rebuttals to pro-abortion arguments. That has been done, and effectively, many times.* What is important when reviewing the history of the abortion movement, however, is a recognition of the fact that many of the justifications for legalized abortion were not simply erroneous, but *deliberate fabrications*. We now know this, because the past several decades have produced a number of prominent defectors from the abortion cause, and those defectors have laid out precisely how the abortion movement duped the public.

Dr. Bernard Nathanson was one of these defectors,** and he was as high-ranking as they come. With infamous abortion champion Lawrence Lader, who died unrepentant in 2006 at the age of 86, Nathanson planned an abortion blitzkrieg. He related their strategy in his memoir *The Hand of God*:

---

* *Embryo: A Defence of Human Life* by Robert P. George, *Pro-Life Answers to Pro-Choice Questions* by Randy Alcorn, and *Love Unleashes Life: Abortion and the Art of Communicating Truth* by my former colleague Stephanie Gray are three great examples of must-have resources.

** Dr. Bernard Nathanson has written a number of essential memoirs and exposes of the abortion movement, including *Aborting America*, *The Abortion Papers: Inside The Abortion Mentality*, and *The Hand of God: A Journey from Death to Life by the Abortion Doctor Who Changed His Mind.* His film showing an abortion procedure, *The Silent Scream*, can be found on YouTube.

> By 1969, we were setting the agenda for a meeting of the leading national pro-abortion figures to take place in Chicago. Out of that meeting would emerge the fledgling National Association for the Repeal of Abortion Laws (NARAL), later changed to the National Abortion Rights Action League, and currently styling itself as the National Abortion and Reproductive Rights Action League. We were putting out feelers to Betty Friedan and her corps of feminists to join us in the revolution, coalition building with the Woodstock nation, and crushing the dinosaurs in the movement who would settle for watered-down measures…Lader, I, and a handful of others such as Howard Moody, then pastor of the Judson Memorial Church in Manhattan's Greenwich Village, were the radicals, the Bolsheviks. We would settle for nothing less than striking down all existing abortion statutes and substituting abortion on demand.[79]

An atheist, Nathanson practiced what he preached. He soon presided over the largest freestanding abortion clinic in the world, operating in Manhattan. "It had," says Nathanson, "10 operating rooms, 35 doctors, 85 nurses. It operated seven days a week, from 8 a.m. to midnight. We did 120 abortions every day in that clinic. At the end of the two years that I was the director, we had done 60,000 abortions. I myself, with my own hands, have done 5,000 abortions. I have supervised another 10,000 that residents have done under my direction. So I have 75,000 abortions in my lifetime."[80] Two of those abortions were Dr. Nathanson's own children.

It was not Nathanson's confessions of being an efficient and prolific abortionist that stunned both sides of the abortion debate when, in the mid-1970s, he began to explore the fledgling field of fetology and came to the sickening realization that he had been accomplice to the mass killing of developing human beings. It was his revelations concerning how brazenly the abortion movement had lied to the public. Slogans that had captured the public imagination and sprung from the lips of thousands of protestors: "freedom of choice," "My body, my choice," and a score of other mindless chants had been invented with derisive chuckles at those who adopted them with vigor. "I remember laughing when we made those slogans up," Nathanson revealed. "We were looking for some sexy, catchy slogans to capture public opinion. They were very cynical slogans then, just as all of these slogans today are very, very cynical."[81*]

These slogans were designed for a very specific purpose: to shift the abortion debate away from *what was being chosen*—a gruesome procedure that was very difficult to sell to the public—to *choice*, a lovely word that seemed to symbolize all that was good about Western democracy. Abortion activists didn't particularly want to discuss the nitty-gritty details of abortion. They wanted to discuss the so-called right to *choose* abortion.[**]

Following that, NARAL set out to convince the public that abortion was essential. More than that, they said, most people already thought so:

> We persuaded the media that the cause of permissive abortion was a liberal, enlightened, sophisticated one… knowing that if a true poll were taken, we would be soundly defeated, we simply fabricated the results of fictional polls. We announced to the media that we had taken polls and that 60 percent of Americans were in favor of permissive abortion. This is the tactic of the self-fulfilling lie. Few people care to be in the minority. We aroused enough sympathy to sell our program of permissive abortion by fabricating the number of illegal abortions done annually in the US. The actual figure was approaching 100,000, but the figure we gave to

* Nearly every single one of the hundreds of times I've interacted with abortion protestors, their signs and their chants feature precisely the same slogans first invented by the fledgling abortion movement nearly fifty years ago.

** In fact, one of the reasons that abortion remains such a controversial topic is because the pro-life movement often tries to fight this clever pivot. According to Frances Kissling of Catholics for a Free Choice and Kate Michelman, a former leader of NARAL, writing in the *Los Angeles Times* in 2008: "In recent years, the anti-abortion movement successfully put the nitty-gritty details of abortion procedures on public display, increasing the belief that abortion is serious business and that some societal involvement is appropriate." When the debate is about choice, abortion activists win. But when the debate is about *abortion*, pro-lifers often win.

> the media repeatedly was 1 million.* Repeating the big lie often enough convinces the public. The number of women dying from illegal abortions was around 200-500 annually. The figure we constantly fed to the media was 10,000. These false figures took root in the consciousness of Americans, convincing many that we needed to crack the abortion law.[82]

Dr. Bernard Nathanson switched sides and eventually even converted to the Catholic Church, the very one he and Lawrence Lader had once successfully demonized as responsible for the deaths of women who obtained back alley abortions. He became a fierce pro-life advocate, creating films such as *The Silent Scream* and *The Eclipse of Reason*, which exposed the gruesome reality of the abortion procedure and were seen by millions.

When the Canadian abortion movement began to use arguments that he himself had invented to push for the removal of all abortion restrictions, Dr. Nathanson went on TV in March of 1983 to debate Dr. Henry Morgentaler. Surgically and skillfully, Nathanson dismembered Morgentaler's arguments, reducing the Canadian abortionist to a spluttering fury. At one point, Morgentaler admitted that he and his wife regretted the abortion they had procured during medical school and agreed with the host that the abortion industry was a business filled with "much sorrow." As Morgentaler angrily denounced Nathanson, who calmly pointed out that he actually had more experience in the abortion industry than Morgentaler himself did, Nathanson cut to the chase: "You are not a physician, Dr. Morgentaler. You are an abortionist."**

Nathanson was not alone in his belated discovery of the truth. In 1994, a middle-aged Texas woman named Norma McCorvey announced that she was repudiating her support for the abortion industry. This was remarkable, for a number of reasons. For one,

---

* Even today, debating abortion on university campuses in both Canada and the United States, I have this number thrown at me by angry abortion activists. This is a lie with a very long shelf life.

** A number of segments of the March 1983 debate between Dr. Bernard Nathanson and Dr. Henry Morgentaler on the CHCH television program *Cherington* can still be found on YouTube.

McCorvey had worked in an abortion clinic for many years. She had seen babies in freezers, and had witnessed the banal horrors of day-to-day work in an abortion business. But more importantly, Norma McCorvey was known to the American public as Jane Roe, the infamous "Roe" in *Roe v. Wade*.*

It turned out that Norma McCorvey had been used by abortion activists and attorneys Linda Coffee and Sarah Weddington as a helpful pawn in their drive to bring a good abortion case to challenge the Texas prohibitions on the procedure. McCorvey, then identifying as a lesbian, had gotten pregnant for the third time at age 21 in 1969, and sought an illegal abortion. Weddington and Coffee met with McCorvey. She lied and said she'd been raped. They convinced her to sign on to their case, the case that would eventually become *Roe v. Wade*. It is an irony that the very abortion laws *Roe v. Wade* was intended to overturn were the very laws that saved the life of McCorvey's baby, who was born long before the Supreme Court ruling and given up for adoption.

It was a poster of pre-born babies in the womb hanging inside the office of Operation Rescue near the abortion clinic in which she worked that changed Norma McCorvey's mind. Staring at the little humans on the poster, she realized that none of the "pro-choice" slogans could erase the reality of what she was staring at. Soon, she sought out pro-life activists with Operation Rescue, and began her journey into the pro-life movement. Her resulting memoirs revealed, in excruciating detail, how the very case that had legalized abortion had been based on a lie—that she'd been sexually assaulted—in the first place. Almost nothing about the legalization of abortion, it seems, was truthful.

The same is true for those who run the abortion businesses. In her memoir *The Scarlet Lady: Confessions of A Successful Abortionist*,** Carol Everett lays out how merchants of death made their millions. When I interviewed her in 2016, she told me that the catalyst for her becoming an abortion worker was

* Norma McCorvey has written two memoirs detailing her life and conversion to the pro-life cause, *I am Roe* and *Won By Love*.

** This book was re-released in 1992 with the title *Blood Money: Getting Rich Off a Woman's Right to Choose*.

the same reason so many other women have: her own abortion, which haunted her almost from the day it happened. She became a lethally effective abortion saleswoman. "We were telemarketers," she told me. "Abortion became the only answer. We weren't really counseling, we were telemarketers."

Selling abortion was a simple matter of utilizing streamlined extermination methods and taking advantage of the glories of carnivorous capitalism:

> We opened our clinic and the first month we did 45 abortions. The last month I was there, with two clinics functioning in the Dallas area, we did over 500 abortions a month in that clinic. I was compensated at the rate of $25.00 per case plus one-third of the clinics, so you can imagine what my motivation was. I sold abortions.
>
> I had made $150,000; was on target in 1983 to make $260,000; and when we opened our five clinics, I would have been taking home about a million dollars a year. I expected to make more than that after we were functioning…
>
> I'm sure you've seen those numbers advertised that say "Problem Pregnancy," "Abortion Information," or "Pregnant?". When a young girl finds out she is pregnant, she may not want an abortion, she may just want information. But when she calls that number that's paid for by abortion money, what kind of information do you think she is going to get? Remember, they sell abortions. They don't sell keeping the baby. They don't sell giving the baby up. They don't sell delivering the baby in any form. They only sell abortions.
>
> The counselor that the girl speaks to on the telephone is paid to be her friend. She is supposed to seduce her into a friendship of sorts to sell her the abortion. There are usually two questions the girls ask. The first is: Does it hurt? "Oh, no. Your uterus is a muscle. It's a cramp to open it: a cramp to close it; it's a slight cramping sensation. Everybody's had cramps—every woman in the world." Then they ask: Is it a baby? "No, it's product

> of conception; it's a blood clot; it's a piece of tissue."
>
> When the girl goes in for the abortion she pays up front, then goes into a room for counseling. They give her a 6 to 12-page form. This form is written by an abortion attorney to confuse the girl to death. It works and she doesn't ask any questions. She goes back to the two questions: Does it hurt? Is it a baby?
>
> I cannot tell you one thing that happens in an abortion clinic that is not a lie.[83]

Worse, Everett revealed, abortion business owners like herself utilized sex education in schools, much like Planned Parenthood does now, to encourage risky sexual behavior. The condoms they distributed were cheap condoms, she said, ones that were more likely to break. The birth control was what they called "low dose." That way, pregnancy would occur more often, and the abortion business would be booming.

Carol Everett eventually left the abortion industry, and like Dr. Bernard Nathanson before her, was welcomed into the arms of the pro-life movement. Like those before her, she now spends her time exposing the foundation of lies and propaganda that gave rise to legal abortion and fuel the abortion industry.

Abortion as infanticide

Since the very beginning, pro-life activists have been warning that abortion is no different than infanticide. A culture that permits the destruction of vulnerable human beings within the womb, they have pointed out to largely deaf ears, has abandoned the moral framework necessary to condemn the destruction of vulnerable infants just outside the womb. Especially where abortions are being perpetrated on children who could survive outside the womb, a benchmark moving ever earlier in pregnancy with the advance of medical technology, abortionists are increasingly finding themselves in the position of wondering what to do when a child survives the abortion procedure and is born, to the horror of the attending exterminators. There's even a name for this complication. It's called "live birth."

Consider that for just a moment. In our schizophrenic abortion regime, one set of doctors and nurses work desperately to ensure "live birth," resulting in a healthy boy or girl to place into the arms of joyful parents. Another set of doctors and nurses work desperately to avoid this end, doing their utmost to destroy the developing child in order to give his or her parents the news: *"Congratulations, it's dead!"*

During my travels across North America as a pro-life activist, I've had many nurses tell me of incidents where children were born alive during an attempted abortion. One Canadian nurse recalled the doctor hastily tossing the tiny child into a trash can, where she heard the baby rustling weakly among the papers before he died. Former nurse and current pro-life activist Jill Stanek, whose testimony later helped to pass the Partial-Birth Abortion Ban Act signed into law by George W. Bush in 2003, described how children born alive after failed abortions would be left in the soiled utility room of Christ Hospital in Oak Lawn, Illinois:

> To commit induced labor abortion, a doctor or resident inserts a medication into the mother's birth canal close to the cervix. The cervix is the opening at the bottom of the uterus that normally stays closed until a mother is about 40 weeks pregnant and ready to deliver. This medication irritates the cervix and stimulates it to open early. When this occurs, the small second or third trimester pre-term, fully formed baby falls out of the uterus, sometimes alive. By law, if an aborted baby is born alive, both birth and death certificates must be issued. Ironically, at Christ Hospital the cause of death often listed for live aborted babies is "extreme prematurity," an acknowledgement by doctors that they have caused this death.[84]

These babies can often live on for hours, Stanek revealed. Some of them, aborted healthy, live longer than others. Even in these circumstances, where it is so clear that a human being has been murdered, hospital staff attempts to normalize the experience:

> In the event that an aborted baby is born alive, she or he receives "comfort care," defined as keeping the baby warm in a blanket until s/he dies. Parents may hold the baby if

> they wish. If the parents do not want to hold their dying aborted baby, a staff member cares for the baby until s/he dies. If staff did not have the time or desire to hold the baby, s/he is taken [to] Christ Hospital's new Comfort Room, which is complete with a First Foto Machine if parents want professional pictures of their aborted baby, baptismal supplies, gowns, and certificates, foot printing equipment and baby bracelets for mementos, and a rocking chair. Before the Comfort Room was established, babies were taken to the Soiled Utility Room to die.[85]

One experience stands out starkly in Stanek's mind:

> One night, a nursing co-worker was taking a Down's syndrome baby who was aborted alive to our Soiled Utility Room because his parents did not want to hold him, and she did not have time to hold him. I could not bear the thought of this suffering child dying alone in a Soiled Utility Room, so I cradled and rocked him for the 45 minutes that he lived. He was between 21 and 22 weeks old, weighed about 1/2 pound, and was about 10 inches long. He was too weak to move very much, expending any energy he had trying to breathe. Toward the end he was so quiet that I could not tell if he was still alive. I held him up to the light to see through his chest wall whether his heart was still beating. After he was pronounced dead, we folded his little arms across his chest, wrapped him in a tiny shroud, and carried him to the hospital morgue where all of our dead patients are taken.[86]

Some of these children miraculously survive. I met Melissa Ohden in 2013 outside an abortion clinic in Washington, D.C., at a rally organized by Live Action, a pro-life organization run by the undercover investigator Lila Rose. Rose's organization had just revealed their most recent project, which exposed the routine practice of infanticide among late-term abortion providers. For Ohden, this was personal. She survived a saline infusion abortion in 1977, despite soaking in the womb for days in a solution intended to kill her. When I interviewed her for my radio show in 2016, she told me that she is not the only one. One by one, abortion survivors are contacting her to tell her their stories and share with her the impact the abortion attempts have had on their lives. They are often a group without a voice. After all, according to the law, they should be dead.

Infanticide has been present in the abortion industry since the very beginning, but one recent case has truly highlighted that connection: the 2013 case of Dr. Kermit Gosnell of Philadelphia. His trial put the gruesome reality of the abortion industry on display for all to see, after he was accused of killing a patient through overdose of anesthesia as well as killing possibly hundreds of full-term infants by "snipping," a practice in which he thrust scissors into the backs of their necks and cut their spinal cords. He expressed confusion as to why he was being charged for ending the lives of these children. In his view, he was just performing abortions—and finishing them a little late.

Investigators found around jars on a shelf in Kermit Gosnell's office, each containing fetal parts, many of which were severed feet. Other corpses were, for reasons unknown, stored in milk jugs, juice containers, or dumped into the freezer in bags. Assistant DA Joanne Pescatore speculated that these human body parts could constitute Gosnell's "trophies."

Clinic worker Sherry West, who says she called the babies "specimens" to make the killing process easier, recalled one incident where an infant was born alive, and she was called over to assist in dispatching the child: "There was this clear glass pan, and I saw it, and I thought, 'What do you expect me to do?' It wasn't fully developed. It didn't have eyes or a mouth but it was likes [sic] screeching, making this noise. It was weird. It sounded like a little alien…It really freaked me out, and I said call Dr. Gosnell, and I went back out front."

Clinic worker Lynda Williams, who told the court that snipping the necks of newborn infants was "standard procedure," described how Gosnell trained her to flip the infants over and then swiftly thrust the scissors into the baby's neck and snip his or her spinal cord. She recounted one instance where an infant was delivered into a toilet, and she quickly snipped his or her neck. "It jumped, the arm…" she said.

Steven Massof, who worked for Gosnell for nine years, painted a savage picture of routine inside the clinic: "It would rain fetuses, fetuses and blood all over the place. I felt like a fireman in Hell. I couldn't put out all the fires."

Clinic worker Kareema Cross also testified of the abortion barbarism. According to the grand jury report: "After the baby was expelled, Cross noticed that he was breathing, though not for long. After about 10 to 20 seconds, while the mother was asleep, 'the doctor just slit the neck,' said Cross. Gosnell put the boy's body in a shoebox. Cross described the baby as so big that his feet and arms hung out over the sides of the container. Cross said that she saw the baby move after his neck was cut, and after the doctor placed it in the shoebox. Gosnell told her, 'it's the baby's reflexes. It's not really moving.'" Gosnell, apparently in an attempt to lighten the mood, joked that the baby was big enough to walk him to the bus stop.

Adrienne Moton, one of Gosnell's medical assistants, testified that one 24-week-old baby was born alive into a toilet, and she quickly slit "Baby D's" neck to complete the procedure.

On April 29, 2013, I attended the final day of what had already been dubbed "The Abortion Trial of the Century," and witnessed with faint nausea the prosecutor bravely try to explain why an abortionist was being put on trial for doing his job: killing babies. Abortion wasn't illegal, but infanticide was. Dr. Gosnell didn't see the difference. "This trial," assistant District Attorney Edward Cameron, who had the task of prosecuting Gosnell, informed the court at the outset of his closing arguments, "is not about abortion."

The next two hours, it turned out, were almost entirely about abortion. Cameron pointed out that 54 prosecution witnesses had damned Gosnell's career as an incredibly inept and barbaric tenure of botched butchery—the "standard practice" of slashing the necks of wriggling, mewling newborns, for example. One of the babies born in Gosnell's "House of Horrors" was born alive at 29.5 weeks, and Gosnell's assistant called him in a panic. Gosnell rushed to the clinic—and the child promptly disappeared. "That baby would have been four and a half years old," Cameron said, "I wish to God there was something we could do so it could walk through that door. But it had scissors jammed in its neck, and suffocated to death." He pointed at a steel basin sitting on a table in front of the courtroom. "Babies *do* feel pain—you stick something in them, they'll react. Babies were delivered into this metal pan while the doctor was out, and left to die."

To my right, Gosnell's bored face began to take shape on a court reporter's placard. Cameron pulled up the next slide. It was an abbreviated quote from witness Dr. Karen Feusilin: "Babies never allowed to be born alive—Abortion 101." Cameron paused. "Maybe that's not the best way to put it," he said uncomfortably—and the cat, as it were, was out of the bag screeching and clawing. The trial *was* about abortion—more than that, it was a stark and gruesomely perfect microcosm of our cultural schizophrenia that stipulates that if you want to kill someone, it's all about location, location, location. Cameron only had one thing to quickly add to Feusilin's blunt assessment of Gosnell's legal troubles: "If they are born alive, and you do anything to speed up their death, you are guilty of murder."

Cameron's next point, too, seemed to slip out of his mouth by accident, as he mocked defence attorney Jack McMahon's assertion that a billboard in Gosnell's clinic featuring "happy patients" revealed his scissor-less sweet side: "Abortion patients don't send pictures of kids," he pointed out. On the jury bench, jaws dropped. The tension was fleeting, but palpable. Again, Cameron seemed to realize what he had said and moved on, attempting a recovery by pointing at a graphic photo of post-utero murder victim "Baby Manning": "That's a baby, not a fetus," he asserted lamely.

Quickly re-establishing his assertion that this trial was "not about abortion" by highlighting the testimony of an abortion doctor, Cameron brought up the assertions of a Planned Parenthood abortionist named only as "Dr. Benjamin." Dr. Benjamin, who had the good sense to dismember his victims prior to their forcible eviction, was the perfect example of someone whom Gosnell should have looked up to: "Never was a baby born alive with a heartbeat—because he did things the right way." His follow-up, again, defeated the point: "This nameless baby was one of the many killed by this man. We'll never know who they were, or what they could've done." As opposed to Benjamin's some 40,000 victims, who apparently we were supposed to believe had no future whatsoever beyond a suction aspirator, a medical waste container, and cremation.

The horrific details kept coming, from a baby delivered into a toilet and attempting to swim, to toilets backed up with baby parts (the word "fetus" mysteriously absent from Cameron's vocabulary at this point.) I almost felt sorry for Cameron when he had to defend Pennsylvania's 24-hour waiting period prior to an abortion while maintaining support for abortion. The woman needs a chance to decide whether she "wants to keep the baby," he told the jury, because "When the baby is done… er…when the *abortion* is done, it's done." One woman who attempted to change her mind but had her qualms ignored by Gosnell regrets her abortion to this day—because, Cameron pointed out, "This doctor wouldn't take the time to tell her what abortion is and what it does to the fetus." Cameron cleared up any ambiguity the courtroom had about this a few moments later: "The proper way to do abortions is under anesthesia and the…baby…is manually removed."

Cameron finished with a speech that sounded like something from a pro-life rally, calling Kermit Gosnell the captain of an abortion hell. "Baby after baby after baby…" he pleaded with the jury, "Be their voice."

I remember sitting there, stunned. I agreed with almost everything Edward Cameron had so passionately articulated. I think he even understood what a bizarre position he'd been placed in. Dr. Kermit Gosnell's trial, which resulted in a prison sentence that will ensure he dies behind bars, perfectly illustrated a very simple fact: To the abortion industry, there is little to no difference between abortion and infanticide. Infanticide, in fact, can be more convenient.

In Canada, too, legal abortion has resulted in infanticide. On April 13, 2005, 19-year-old Katrina Effert secretly gave birth to a baby boy in her parent's home. She then strangled the child with her underwear and tossed the corpse over the fence into the yard of one of the neighbours. On September 9, 2011, the CBC reported that Ms. Effert's conviction for this murder had been 'downgraded' by an Edmonton Court of Queen's Bench judge to infanticide, and in lieu of jail time she will merely serve a suspended sentence. In her argument, the judge stated that "while many Canadians undoubtedly view abortion as a less than ideal solution to unprotected sex and unwanted pregnancy, they generally understand, accept, and sympathize with the onerous demands pregnancy and childbirth exact from mothers, especially mothers without support."[87]

Translation? Katrina Effert simply engaged in a really, really late-term abortion. Given that Canadian law does not value human life a few minutes before birth, why a few minutes after?

Indeed, the Abortion Rights Coalition of Canada, run by the virulently pro-abortion Joyce Arthur, posted the CBC article on their Facebook page with the heading: "A tragic situation, but yes, there are compelling reasons for infanticide being a lesser crime than murder."

Canada's politicians have acquiesced to this view with their silence. When it was revealed in 2012 by Statistics Canada that 491 babies had been born alive and left to die after abortions between 2000 and 2009, pro-life activists called for an official police investigation. When questioned about this in the House of Commons, then-Prime Minister Stephen Harper responded by stating that, "All members of this House, whether they agree with it or not, understand that abortion is legal in Canada and this government, myself included, have made it very clear that the government does not intend to change the law in this regard."

In 2015, LifeSiteNews reported that, "according to official data from Statistics Canada, as many as 182 babies died after they were born alive following late-term abortions in 2013-14, a 16 percent increase over 2011-12." Again, requests for an investigation were ignored.[88]

In both Canada and the United States, politicians, prosecutors, and the public have proven time and time again that they see the victims of infanticide as the collateral damage of a legal abortion industry.

Our killer culture

Abortion activists have long since abandoned the purring reassurances of old guard feminists like Hillary Clinton, who assured us that abortion should remain "safe, legal, and rare." Instead, the ideologies of the Sexual Revolution have been utilized by eugenicists* and monetized by big business to create a human throwaway culture that has made abortion sacred, lethal, and frequent. The abortion movement no longer pretends that abortion is a "necessary evil" to be used in extreme circumstances. They never believed that anyway, of course. Now, they launch campaigns asking women to tell their abortion stories (even featuring a repulsive hashtag #ShoutYourAbortion) in order to normalize the procedure, with many abortion workers admitting, quite frankly, that abortion ends the life of a human being, and that they don't think it matters.** Abortion as a form of birth control is standard.

Abortion is now used to weed out human beings our society finds imperfect or inconvenient. It often takes the form of cruel ableism, with abortion rates of babies who test positive for Down syndrome ranging from 60% to over 90% across the Western world. The potential of disability or deformity has always been used as a perverse justification for abortion, and is now a common motivation for the procedure. Pro-life activists in both Canada and the United States have heard of late-term abortions for reasons as trivial as cleft palate and other correctible conditions that derelict parents simply cannot be bothered to deal with. This eugenic mindset has even led to the rise of "wrongful birth" lawsuits, in which parents who

---

* The history of the eugenics movement will be examined in Chapter 6.

** Hanna Rosin, journalist and author of *The End of Men and the Rise of Women*, joined one of these campaigns in 2014, writing about her abortion in on Slate.com. "Part of me thinks the shadow aborted child stayed with me and created a space for the last one to be born," she wrote. It is interesting to note that she makes no attempt to deny it is a child.

claim they would have aborted their son or daughter had they known of the disabilities their child would have actually sue medical professionals for not alerting them in time to opt for termination.* Dozens of these cases have already succeeded in court, with our culture sending a loud and clear message to the despised survivors: *You should be dead right now.*

The new mantra of the abortion movement now rings out loud and clear: *There is no such thing as a bad abortion.* Canadian abortion activists were not even shaken by revelations that gender-selection abortion, in which parents opt to abort daughters due to preferences (often cultural) for sons, takes place in some communities. If that is what the woman wants, the feminists announced, then that is what she shall have.

While our society has abandoned its respect for human life, its relentless regard for practices such as recycling has not wavered. Investigations by organizations such as Life Dynamics and the Center for Medical Progress have revealed the fate of the tiny corpses of some abortion victims:

> Although marketing fetal tissue is a violation of federal law, a major loophole and a carefully devised scheme by abortion industry insiders has allowed for a profitable and growing industry in the sale of baby body parts. Using a "wholesaler," who can best be described as a middleman between researchers (at medical schools, pharmaceutical companies, bio-tech companies or government agencies, etc.) and the abortion clinics, requests for certain body parts are made, harvested, and "donated". In this process the wholesaler pays a "site fee" to the clinic and is reimbursed for the cost of retrieving the parts.[89]

These revelations, first in 1997 from Life Dynamics and again in 2015 from the Center for Medical Progress, did not shake the resolve of the feminist Frankensteins in the slightest. In response to undercover videos that showed Planned Parenthood employees bargaining over baby hearts, livers, and brains and even featured one technician describe snipping through a baby

* LifeSiteNews.com and other pro-life as well as secular news outlets feature dozens of these sickening stories.

boy's face to harvest his brain while his heart was still beating, they simply shrugged and protested that donating aborted children to research firms was perfectly legal. One cadaver dealer chuckled to undercover investigator David Daleiden that they did have to warn the researchers whenever they were sending cases of intact children to the lab to ensure that the researchers would not be startled, presumably by spasms of conscience. These little humans are not considered human enough to merit human rights. They are, however, human enough to have their corpses pillaged for human research.

The pro-life movement in the 21st century

In spite of all of this, the pro-life movement in both Canada and the United States is thriving. In the United States, each new year brings more pro-life laws on the state level, leading *Slate* columnist Michelle Goldberg to call 2015, which saw 57 pro-life laws pass, "the worst for abortion rights in America since *Roe v. Wade* was decided 42 years ago." In addition to this and in large part due to relentless activism and undercover campaigns by pro-life groups, 53 abortion clinics closed their doors.

Abortion activists are prone to express disbelief that decades after they assumed the abortion question was settled, the pro-life movement continues to grow and come up with new, creative ways to impact the culture and increase support for laws protecting life in the womb. It's a sentiment that often shows up on their incredulous, petulant signs at protest rallies: "I can't believe I still have to protest this s**t."

This state of affairs has worried abortion activists, and led former NARAL chief Nancy Keenan to step down in 2012 in hopes that younger activists would step in to fill her place. This was after she expressed fear about the resurgence of the pro-life movement in a *Newsweek* article in 2010:

> And what worries Keenan is that she just doesn't see a passion among the post-*Roe* generation—at least, not among those on her side. This past January, when Keenan's train pulled into Washington's Union Station, a few blocks from the Capitol, she was greeted by a

> swarm of anti-abortion-rights activists. It was the 37th annual March for Life, organized every year on Jan. 22, the anniversary of Roe. "I just thought, my gosh, they are so young," Keenan recalled. "There are so many of them, and they are so young." March for Life estimates it drew 400,000 activists to the Capitol this year.[90]

It turns out that a movement founded to kill the youngest members of the human family is having a difficult time recruiting the youth.

Canada's pro-life movement is also seeing a resurgence of youth involvement that has not gone unnoticed by the mainstream media. The *Toronto Star*, Canada's largest and most liberal newspaper, reported in 2012 that the pro-life movement was changing and growing. The Canadian Centre for Bio-Ethical Reform, where I serve as communications director, has seen staff numbers grow from around five to over fifty in five short years, with millions of Canadians per year being exposed to the reality of what abortion does to children in the womb. Every single day, boots hit the ground on Canadian streets, campuses, and other public spaces. Every single day, pro-life activists witness minds being changed, hearts being softened, and lives being saved.

It is a truly humbling experience to sit down with university students who want to change their career plans—their *life* plans, really—from doctor, lawyer, or teacher, and instead want to join the pro-life movement fulltime. They understand what sort of culture legal abortion has created, and they rebel against it. They are the new counter-culture.

One of the most moving things I have ever seen was a room packed full of beautiful, smiling girls and guys, sunburnt from days of outdoor summer pro-life outreach, grinning at a small laptop screen with smiles so big their faces must have hurt. They were watching a tiny pre-born child wave her arms and legs on an ultrasound, and listening to the tiny *thomp-thomp, thomp-thomp* of her heart emanating from the computer speakers.

You see, her mother had planned to abort her—until she met pro-life activists on the streets, holding pictures of abortion victims, showing the culture truth in a time when lies are all the rage. Her child did not end up in a biohazard bucket in a hospital backroom or in a dumpster behind an abortion clinic. Her baby was born several months later in a Canadian hospital and placed into the waiting arms of her mother. The baby girl's name is Ava, and she is alive.

Those who stand up in defence of life have always faced challenges. Many of them have seemed insurmountable, and societies drunk on the blood of the innocents have often pushed back angrily and violently. But the pro-life tradition continues, and the life-saving work goes on.

Chapter 6

Euthanasia and Eugenics

Most Eugenists are Euphemists. I mean merely that short words startle them, while long words soothe them. And they are utterly incapable of translating the one into the other, however obviously they mean the same thing. Say to them "The persuasive and even coercive powers of the citizen should enable him to make sure that the burden of longevity in the previous generation does not become disproportionate and intolerable, especially to the females"; say this to them and they will sway slightly to and fro like babies sent to sleep in cradles. Say to them "Murder your mother," and they sit up quite suddenly. Yet the two sentences, in cold logic, are exactly the same.

—G.K. Chesterton, *Eugenics and Other Evils*

We once lived in a culture that drafted laws to protect "dependents": the very young, the very old, and the disabled. This was done in recognition of the fact that the increased vulnerability of a human being correspondingly heightens our moral responsibility to that human being.

Now, however, the exit strategists of the Sexual Revolution are burning the candle at both ends—on one end, abortion for children in the womb; on the other, euthanasia and "assisted suicide" for the old, the mentally ill, and the disabled. Both children and elderly parents can be costly and time-consuming. The concept of "dying with dignity" is rapidly becoming "killing with impunity," as our culture finds all sorts of excuses to assist inconvenient people in leaving Planet Earth.

Here too, there is a similarity to abortion—our technologically advanced culture is no longer looking for compassionate and ethical solutions to complex, tragic, and often heartbreaking circumstances. Instead, we offer the solution that Darkness always offers: Death. Disability, dependence, difficult life circumstances. A suction aspirator, a lethal injection, a bloody set of forceps. The "problem," as it were, is solved. We don't kill problems anymore. We kill people, and pretend that it is the same thing.

The connection between abortion and euthanasia is closer than one might think. As Canada began to implement euthanasia in 2016, one of the first people killed was a Calgary, Alberta woman suffering from ALS. She flew to Vancouver, British Columbia—because while many physicians were protesting the legalization of euthanasia, Dr. Ellen Wiebe, the director of the Willow Women's abortion clinic, was happy to do the deed, and announced that her clinic would be willing to provide such services in the future as well. Dispatching human beings, after all, was already her job description.

There is something chilling about the intimacy of these killings. As pro-life activist Gregg Cunningham noted, "Ours is the first generation that, having demanded the right to kill its children through elective abortion, is now demanding the right to kill its parents through doctor-assisted suicide." The closest of human relationships are rupturing under the sheer weight of the selfishness and narcissism of the Me Generation. In fact, the tagline "dying with dignity" is starting to very much sound like, "Now don't make a fuss, off with you now." Consider this 2014 story in *The Daily Mail*:

> An elderly husband and wife have announced their plans to die in the world's first 'couple' euthanasia - despite neither of them being terminally ill.
>
> Instead the pair fear loneliness if the other one dies first from natural causes.
>
> Identified only by their first names, Francis, 89, and Anne, 86, they have the support of their three adult children who say they would be unable to care for either parent if they became widowed.
>
> The children have even gone so far as to find a practitioner willing to carry out the double killings

> on the grounds that the couple's mental anguish constituted the unbearable suffering needed to legally justify euthanasia...
>
> The couple's daughter has remarked that her parents are talking about their deaths as eagerly as if they were planning a holiday.
>
> John Paul [their son] said the double euthanasia of his parents was the 'best solution'.
>
> 'If one of them should die, who would remain would be so sad and totally dependent on us,' he said. 'It would be impossible for us to come here every day, take care of our father or our mother.'[91]

I wonder why no one considers the fact that the reason some elderly parents may experience "mental anguish" is that they have come to the sickening realization that their grown children would rather find an executioner to dispatch them than take on the responsibility of caring for their parents.

It is for precisely that reason that some scenes in the 2011 HBO euthanasia documentary *How To Die In Oregon* are so jarring. In one scene, an elderly father explains to the interviewer why he has procured death drugs that he plans to take in case of severe health problems. "I don't want to be a burden," he explains while his adult daughter nods approvingly, "It's the decent thing to do. For once in my life I'll do something decent."

There was no argument from his daughter.

Culling the weak

The growing cultural acceptance of euthanasia, as with abortion and infanticide, is not new. Cultures throughout human history have cruelly dispatched the weak and the disabled, and unwanted children have been aborted or left to die in many bygone civilizations. What is different this time around is that we are rejecting the centuries-old consensus, based on Judeo-Christian principles, that all human life has value. We are not discovering barbarism and the capacity for callous killing so much as we are rediscovering it, and returning to pre-Christian practices rooted this time not in paganism, but in post-modernism.

As much as humanists would like to protest this fact, it was the rise of the evolutionary theory of natural selection, propagated by Charles Darwin and his acolytes, that first began to erode the foundational belief that all human life was inherently valuable. After all, if there was no God, then no one was created in His image. If there was no God, then some people *were*, by very definition, defective evolutionary accidents. If there was no God, then there was no reason whatsoever to assume that all human beings were valuable and equal. In fact, the very theory of evolutionary natural selection *precluded* the idea of equality. In the Darwinian view of the human race, equality as anything other than a feeble social construct cannot be possible.

Charles Darwin did not shy from this fact or avoid its conclusions. In his 1882 work *The Descent of Man and Selection in Relation to Sex*, he noted: "With savages, the weak in body or mind are soon eliminated; and those that survive commonly exhibit a vigorous state of health. We civilised men, on the other hand, do our utmost to check the process of elimination; we build asylums for the imbecile, the maimed, and the sick; we institute poor-laws; and our medical men exert their utmost skill to save the life of every one to the last moment. There is reason to believe that vaccination has preserved thousands, who from a weak constitution would formerly have succumbed to small-pox. Thus the weak members of civilised societies propagate their kind. No one who has attended to the breeding of domestic animals will doubt that this must be highly injurious to the race of man. It is surprising how soon a want of care, or care wrongly directed, leads to the degeneration of a domestic race; but excepting in the case of man itself, hardly any one is so ignorant as to allow his worst animals to breed."[92]

What Charles Darwin quite accurately described was a Christian society dedicated to caring for the weakest members of society. What he was decrying, in not so subtle terms, was the fact that the result of Christian charity seemed to him to be a human race containing a significant number of faulty and worthless human beings.

The distinction between so-called "civilized men" and savages soon became difficult to differentiate. With Darwin's theories of natural selection providing the supposedly definitive evidence that human beings were not fundamentally equal and therefore did not need to be treated as such, eugenics became all the rage. God did not make mistakes in creating humans, but natural selection certainly could. This meant that the mentally ill, the handicapped, and the constitutionally weak were not created in God's image. They were defective accidents of nature.

Darwin's cousin, the scientist Francis Galton, dedicated himself to the pursuit of applying Darwin's theory of natural selection to social policy. Ted Byfield's history of Christianity *Unto the Ends of the Earth* describes the dark and cruel movement that sprung up:

> With the publication of Galton's book, *Hereditary Genius*, in 1869, the science of "eugenics" (literally, "good birth") was born and named. Within two decades it was also a "movement," promulgating throughout the occidental world plans for selective breeding of the white race, suppression of the yellow race, and eradication of the black race. Among whites, the less worthy should not be allowed to procreate or even associate with higher stock. Confined to "labor camps," they should be treated benignly, but any violation of the eugenic code would bring a charge of treason. Although most people unsurprisingly felt that Galton had somehow "gone too far," his defenders portrayed any critics as obstructing scientific advance, just as they had tried to obstruct Galileo, they declared. His cousin Charles was exuberantly in favor, however. "I do not think I ever in all my life read anything more interesting and original," he wrote.[93]

Eugenics was never fully embraced in Great Britain, despite it being the birthplace of these ideas. Too many politicians opposed them, many for religious reasons. But the eugenics movement did find great success in the United States and Canada. Harvard zoologist Charles Benedict Davenport, for example, promoted eugenics as a way of reducing the crime rate and creating a moral society. His eugenicist comrade Harry Hamilton Laughlin, the Superintendent of the Eugenics Record Office in New York from 1910 until it closed in 1939, was so fanatic that he actually condemned many charitable organizations. He was willing to admit that they did much for the suffering, but that, in his mind, was a barrier to scientific progress.* His view of what progress actually consisted of was chilling:

> Davenport and Laughlin founded and developed the Eugenics Record Office on Long Island, New York, which over the next thirty years would send out hundreds of young women to compile detailed records on 534,625 Americans whom they deemed to be "defective." Sixty thousand of them would face sterilization, many of the males by compulsory castration. But the eugenicists saw this as barely a beginning. Their initial goal was to sterilize fourteen million people in the United States and millions more worldwide, thus replacing the "lower tenth" of the human race with "pure Nordic stock."[94]

It was not just Davenport and Laughlin, either. Scores of scientists and scholars climbed aboard the grotesque eugenics bandwagon, from the inventor of the telephone, Alexander Graham Bell, to Nobel Prize winner and surgeon, Alexis Carrel.** Attracted to the moralistic overtones of ridding society of criminals and degenerates, and seduced by the supposed scientific underpinnings, liberal clergy members soon began to support the movement as well. Stories of this dark chapter in Western history are often ignored, and it is no surprise. They are a testament to the danger of Darwinism and the inevitable brutality of big government. The United States Supreme Court, for example, upheld state policies of forced sterilization, even in the face of public outcry:

---

* It is interesting to note that one of the largest donors funding the American eugenics movement was the Rockefeller Foundation, which would also fund the work of Dr. Alfred Kinsey several decades later.

** Margaret Sanger, the birth control crusader and founder of Planned Parenthood (now the world's largest abortion provider), also found common cause with the eugenics movement. She used their theories to promote birth control as a means towards a better-bred population.

> Public support for eugenics had never been strong, particularly after the Hearst newspapers launched a campaign against it in 1915 with one horror story after another. Some of these came from far-off Britain where an eight-year-old boy reportedly was castrated when found masturbating, and a fifteen-year-old because he allegedly "rubbed himself" against a woman. After thirty-eight children in one Kansas institution had been surgically sterilized, an inquiry found that the superintendent had violated the law by ordering it, although he was neither charged nor fired. There were heartrending stories from poor farm families of the South who cooperated hospitably with the "nice lady" who came to ask them about their family and then found themselves ordered sterilized by the local board of health. But their son and daughter-in-law had only just been married, they pleaded. Naturally they wanted to have children. That was too bad. Progress was progress.[95]

In Canada too, eugenics spread. The province of Alberta's 1928 Sexual Sterilization Act was intended to reduce the number of undesirable humans, and thus created a Eugenics Board to assist in this endeavor. Similar legislation passed in British Columbia in 1933. These boards possessed an appalling power, and were even permitted to make sterilization contingent for release from a mental institution. Nearly 3,000 sterilizations were carried out, and the Alberta Eugenics Board remained in place until Peter Lougheed's Progressive Conservative government abolished it in 1972. British Columbia's legislation was repealed in 1973. A postscript to Canada's entanglement with social Darwinism came in 1996, when an Alberta court awarded Leilani Muir nearly one million dollars for "wrongful sterilization." She had been sterilized against her will in 1959.

Ironically, it was the Second World War that for the most part halted the eugenics movement. The Nazis embraced eugenics whole-heartedly, and were determined to accelerate the process to create a race of supermen. They would go beyond sterilization—although they certainly practiced that too—to extermination. Initially, eugenicists across the West were thrilled by Nazi ideas. Charles Davenport, for example, had to be told to quell his enthusiasm by financial backers at the Carnegie Foundation, who found his writings in *Eugenics News* in support of Nazi eugenic policies to be rather embarrassing. In 1937, one American eugenicist actually headed to Germany to assist them in their efforts:

> At Buchenwald near Weimar, a prison camp would provide Dr. Edwin Katzen-Ellenbogen, a Polish-born, American-trained eugenicist, with research and other facilities. A founding member of the American Eugenics Research Association, Katzen-Ellenbogen had been chief eugenicist of the State of New Jersey under its former governor, Woodrow Wilson. At Buchenwald, he proceeded to infect some prisoners with typhus to test new drugs. In others he made gland implants with synthetic hormones to observe the physical effects. The camp's program was generously funded by the Rockefeller Foundation, and its files maintained through a system developed by IBM.[96]

Dr. Katzen-Ellenbogen was eventually given a life prison sentence at the Nuremburg trials for his efforts. It was at Nuremburg that the sordid details of the Nazi obsession with eugenics began to come out in their entirety. In fact, the very year that the Eugenics Record Office closed in Long Island, New York, Adolf Hitler initiated the secret T4 Euthanasia Program in Germany. The Nazis had no intention of waiting for handicapped and mentally ill people to be bred out of existence. Along with many elderly people, they dedicated themselves to culling out those who had "lives unworthy of living." Hitler's personal physician, Dr. Karl Brandt, was put in charge of the process.

Seduced by the trash science of eugenics and fueled by ideological fervor, almost the entire psychiatric community in Germany collaborated with the practice of euthanizing patients they deemed unfit to live. The very people who were supposed to be assisting the mentally ill and the handicapped were the very people signing death warrants. Many of them viewed the Nazi ideology as "applied biology," and saw the deaths they assisted or perpetrated as "mercy killings."

Victims selected for execution were starved, lethally injected, or poisoned. After testing the method of gassing patients in chambers disguised as showers, six gas chambers were set up across Germany and Austria as the most effective way of dispatching those selected for death. The infamous SS were put in charge of transporting the victims, and the families of the murdered were dutifully informed of their relatives' passing with a formal death certificate and the ashes of their loved one in an urn. Many had no idea that their family member had not died of natural causes, but was actually killed by physicians appointed by the state to cull the human herd. In only two years, more than 70,000 people were killed by doctors.

The T4 Euthanasia Program was formally discontinued on August 24, 1941, partially in response to the growing voices of protest from the Christian community. But it was a ruse. The killing of those deemed too weak to be worthy of life in the race of Nazi superman continued unabated, with some historians estimating that close to 200,000 people were actually murdered in secret. It is hard to know what the precise number is, because by that point the Nazis were killing people in their millions, slaughtering men, women, children, and families, including Jews, gypsies, Slavs, and countless other groups of people who did not qualify for membership in society due to their lack of "good birth." Instead, the Nazis would give them a terrifying death.

The crimes of the Nazis stunned the world, and the voices of many eugenicists fell silent as the sickening realization dawned on them that eugenics does not begin and end with sterilization. It may start there, yes. But when the theories are wholly and enthusiastically applied, their natural end is the yawning death pits of the Nazi concentration camps, filled with the broken corpses of discarded humanity.

Euthanasia in the Netherlands

Just over half a century later on April 1, 2002, the Netherlands became the first country in Europe since Nazi Germany to legalize euthanasia.

On October 7, 2013, *The Daily Mail* reported that a Dutch woman had been killed by medics via lethal injection because she feared she could not cope with becoming blind. One of the health specialists analyzing her case insisted that it was exceptional because, "She was, for example, obsessed by cleanliness and could not stand being unable to see spots on her clothes."[97]

In 2014, the Euthanasia Prevention Coalition described that the Dutch media had reported another death: "A physically healthy man of 63 who was working for a government institution, died by euthanasia. He never had a relationship and the only thing he did his whole life was work. This man had been treated for a long time for depression, but the treatment didn't work out. He also tried to commit suicide, but he failed. According to psychiatrist Gerty Casteelen this man decided that he wanted to die. The night before his death, he gave a farewell reception for his colleagues. The day after, Casteelen went to his house and gave him a lethal injection."[98]

In 2015, an 80-year-old women was killed by euthanasia against the wishes of her caretakers at the nursing home Ter Reede, where she resided. Her family had petitioned a Dutch court to approve her death, which she could not consent to, due to purportedly suffering from some form of dementia. Her family claimed she would have wanted death, and, despite strong opposition from the management of the nursing home, medical practitioners, and the woman's doctor, an Utrecht judge agreed.

In 2015, a Dutch euthanasia clinic was reprimanded for euthanizing a healthy 47-year-old woman who said that a ringing in her ears—a condition known as tinnitus—was unbearable.

And on and on it goes. The Netherlands, once a bastion of Christianity and a refuge for the persecuted, is now on the cutting edge of medical killing. Euthanasia has been more or less permitted for decades, and the *Termination of Life on Request and Assisted Suicide* has been Dutch law for more than ten years. To understand where legal euthanasia leads, we need only look to the Netherlands. LifeSiteNews correspondent Jeanne Smits reported on the situation in 2014:

For the fifth year in a row, deaths by euthanasia and assisted suicide have risen sharply in the Netherlands. There were 4,829 reported cases in 2013, according to official statistics released yesterday by the five regional control commissions in charge of checking the procedures' compliance with the law.

This amounts to a 15% increase in one year. That number has nearly doubled since 2009 when 2,636 cases were registered. The overwhelming majority of cases was deemed lawful; only five were criticized either because the second doctor consulted before performing the act was not "independent" in these cases, or because the substance used to provoke a coma before administering a muscle relaxant was not the one prescribed by official euthanasia guidelines.

Not a single case will give rise to an official complaint or investigation by the judiciary authorities.

This means that 99.9 percent of all cases of such cases in the nation—4,501 cases of euthanasia, 286 assisted suicides and 42 combinations of the two—met the conditions of the Dutch law.

But how stringent are they? A closer look at the statistics and their rapid increase shows that killing the elderly, the ill and the mentally fragile is becoming socially and medically more acceptable, on ever-widening grounds.

While most voluntary ending of lives involved cancer patients complaining of "unbearable suffering"—3,588 of the total—the most spectacular progression is that of euthanasia on patients with dementia and psychiatric illnesses. In all, 97 persons with incipient or fully developed dementia were killed in 2013; 42 with mental illness, as opposed to 14 in 2012 and 13 the year before that. The statistics indicate that doctors are increasingly accepting loss of autonomy, fear of suffering or humiliation, and despair—sometimes linked to psychological trauma—as acceptable causes for euthanasia.

> In 251 cases, multiple complaints associated with growing old were accepted as a valid reason for euthanasia.
>
> Euthanasia for the demented is one of the main priorities of the "chosen end of life" lobby in the Netherlands. In 2010, the 21 cases approved by the control commissions all concerned people who were becoming demented but still capable of expressing their own will. In fact, they chose to be killed at that stage because the overwhelming majority of doctors [were] not prepared to carry out euthanasia on a person who was no longer able to state and repeat the request while in possession of his free will.
>
> Since then the "Association for voluntary end of life" (NVVE) has lobbied intensely in political circles but also in the field, organizing conferences and meetings to raise public awareness as to this "problem" and to encourage people over 70 to make living wills requesting euthanasia in case dementia would leave them helpless and dependent.[99]

Even these staggering numbers may not be complete as they do not include what is often referred to as "euthanasia by omission," where patients are terminally sedated before being dehydrated and starved to death.

Advocates for euthanasia often promote the practice of medical practitioners killing and assisting in suicide as a carefully regulated, narrow, and guarded path towards so-called "physician-assisted suicide." In not a single jurisdiction in which euthanasia has been legalized have these promises come to pass. Far from it—as the preceding examples illustrate, we're not talking about a narrow, guarded path. We're talking about a four-lane highway with no speed limit.

In fact, even when physicians object to a request for euthanasia, suicidal people have options. *The Daily Mail* reported in 2013 that in March of 2012, "Holland launched the world's first mobile death squads to be dispatched when family doctors refuse to administer lethal drugs on 'ethical' grounds." These units, featuring doctors and nurses willing to administer lethal injections, make up what the BBC called "euthanasia on wheels."[100] Less than one lifetime after the Nazi T-4 euthanasia program was shut down as the result of sustained protests from Christian churches, mobile death units are rolling out into cobble-stoned streets once again.

As a postscript to the grisly story of euthanasia in the Netherlands, it is worth noting that physicians have begun to advocate and implement the practice of harvesting organs from euthanized patients. The medical journal *Applied Cardiopulmonary Pathophysiology* published a description of how this is carried out in 2011:

> Donors were admitted to the hospital a few hours before the planned euthanasia procedure. A central venous line was placed in a room adjacent to the operating room. Donors were heparinized [a drug to maintain organ viability] immediately before a cocktail of drugs was given by the treating physician who agreed to perform the euthanasia. The patient was announced dead on cardiorespiratory criteria by 3 independent physicians as required by Belgian legislation for every organ donor...The deceased was then rapidly transferred, installed on the operating table, and intubated [in preparation for organ removal] ...[101]

Ethicist Wesley J. Smith of the Center for Bioethics and Culture responded with horror.

> Ponder the enormity of what was done here. Four people—who were not otherwise dying—were killed and then swiftly wheeled into a surgery suite to have their organs removed. Three of the donors were struggling with neuromuscular disabilities—people who often face social isolation and discrimination—and one was mentally ill. In a particularly bitter irony, the latter patient was a chronic self-harmer, the "treatment" for which was a willing professional team ready to administer the ultimate harm.
>
> That's just the beginning. Prominent voices among the medical elite have called for the overturning of the "dead donor rule"—the ethical backbone of organ transplant

> medicine requiring that a patient die naturally from injury or illness before vital organs can be procured. These advocates argue that consent should be the primary ethical concern and criteria for organ harvesting—not that a donor is dead. Thus if living patients or their surrogates give the okay, doctors should be allowed to euthanize by means of live harvesting.[102]

Our culture has rejected the sanctity of life, but it seems we're supposed to take comfort from the fact that we have embraced recycling. The hearts of the murdered can pump on in the body of a worthy beneficiary.

The spread of euthanasia

Governments throughout the Western world should have seen the Dutch euthanasia regime as a cautionary tale. Unfortunately, many seem to have taken it as an example to follow. In 2003, Belgium also legalized euthanasia, leapfrogging the Dutch to create the most liberal euthanasia laws in the world. The Netherlands faced a creeping Culture of Death. In Belgium, it moved at a breakneck speed. According to The Witherspoon Institute:

> In order to qualify for euthanasia in Belgium, a person must suffer from acute and "incurable" physical or mental pain. Polls in Belgium show broad support for euthanasia, and the number of cases has grown steadily every year since it was legalized in 2003. In 2003, there were 235 cases of euthanasia. In 2013, there were 1,816. One out of every twenty deaths in Belgium is now deliberately caused. In 2014, Belgium became the first country in the world to legalize euthanasia for children. If you ask to be euthanized in Belgium today, chances are three in four that your request will be granted. Most of Belgium's euthanized patients have terminal cancer, but people are also being euthanized for autism, anorexia, borderline personality disorders, chronic-fatigue syndrome, and depression.[103]

It is safe to say that everyone knows someone who struggles with depression. Most people know someone who has attempted suicide. The idea that someone struggling with mental illness should be assisted in their desire for death should shock and appall people. But in Belgium and other euthanasia countries, the instinct seems to be more along the lines of pushing people out of the window rather than talking them off of the ledge.

In fact, in 2015 PBS actually aired a sympathetic documentary of a young Belgian woman who sought physician-assisted suicide as a way to escape her depression. In one chilling scene, "Eva"—a pseudonym—welcomed suicide practitioner Dr. Marc Van Hoey into her home. By his own estimation, he has already killed more than 100 people over the past 12 years. Eva, dressed in a T-shirt and sweatpants and accompanied by her dog, is eager to die. "Let's get on with this."

Eva lay down on her living room couch, and Dr. Van Hoey knelt down next to her with a needle. "I start with a narcotic drug, in a higher dose, to create a deep sleep. And later on we give barbiturate in a shot. If you use an intravenous injection and do it good, the patient is dead in one or two minutes." He gave her first one injection, and then another. Minutes later, Eva was dead. She was thirty-four years old.

When asked how he felt about killing his patients, Dr. Van Hoey was relaxed. "I am quite used to it," he replied. "It is part of my job."

While euthanasia and assisted suicide remain illegal in many North American jurisdictions, that may not be the case for long. With varying restrictions, assisted suicide is now legal in New Mexico, Oregon, Vermont, Washington, Montana, and California. Canada's Supreme Court overturned all laws criminalizing euthanasia in 2015, and Canadian Parliament passed legislation formalizing euthanasia legalization in 2016. Many euthanasia advocates have now begun to call for the forced participation of physicians as well, demanding that the medical practitioners be forced to provide an "effective referral" if they are unwilling to kill the patient themselves. If these euthanasia advocates have their way, one of the casualties of medical killing will be the healthy consciences of those who refuse to participate.

Euthanasia as infanticide

In 2012, the *Journal of Medical Ethics* published an article titled, "After-birth abortion: why should the baby live?" In it, authors Alberto Giubilini and Francesca Minerva made the case that pro-life activists had been making for years: That fundamentally, there in not difference between abortion and infanticide. One was prenatal infanticide, the other was neonatal infanticide. Ethically speaking, why should a matter of location make much of a difference?

Stories of infants being murdered after surviving an abortion attempt have been leaking out of the abortion industry like blood seeping from beneath a clinic door for as long as abortion has been legal. Since it happens frequently and since there is very little difference between a baby in the womb and a baby outside the womb, these two so-called ethicists proposed that "what we call [an] 'after-birth abortion' (killing a newborn) should be permissible in all the cases where abortion is, including cases where the newborn is not disabled." There was already precedent for killing infants, they wrote: "In The Netherlands, for instance, where the Groningen Protocol (2002) allows to actively terminate the life of 'infants with a hopeless prognosis who experience what parents and medical experts deem to be unbearable suffering.'" The authors refer to this as "euthanasia in infants."

Ethicist Wesley J. Smith calls it something else. He calls it murder:

> Support for infanticide is becoming positively trendy. Where once support for killing babies born with birth defects was a fringe belief, it became respectable—even mainstream—after doctors from Groningen University Medical Center in the Netherlands admitted in 2004 that they euthanized dying and profoundly disabled babies under the terms of what has come to be called the "Groningen Protocol."
>
> The Protocol permits doctors to lethally inject three categories of sick or disabled newborn infants:

> *The baby has no chance of survival (which is sometimes misdiagnosed)*
>
> *The baby "may survive after a period of intensive treatment but expectation for their future are very grim" or,*
>
> *The baby does "not depend on technology for physiologic stability" but whose "suffering is severe, sustained, and cannot be alleviated."*
>
> This means that not only are dying babies lethally injected, but also babies with serious disabilities who do not need intensive care.[104]

This news out of The Netherlands triggered no outcry. Indeed, the reason Smith uses the term "trendy" is because coverage of the Dutch infanticide policy was positively glowing. *The New York Times* published an article lauding Dr. Eduard Verhagen, one of the infanticide movement's most prominent advocates, as a humanitarian. They described the Groningen Protocol as a "Crusade Born of a Suffering Infant's Cry." The *New England Journal of Medicine* allowed two Dutch doctors to explain their quest to "develop norms" for infanticide, greatly legitimizing this endeavour. And one of the most prestigious bioethics journals, the *Hastings Center Report*, published an article called "Ending the Life of a Newborn," in which they made the case for infanticide.

What doctors and ethicists have claimed in the euthanasia debate is the right to kill. With abortion, of course, the medical profession had already claimed the right to take human life, but the lies of so-called pro-choice activists who claimed that abortion does not take a life prevented many from saying this too loudly. With euthanasia, it is entirely different. The debate has been framed to a large extent as promoting the "right-to-die," which is surely the natural conclusion of a society that has rejected God and embraced personal autonomy to the fullest extent. But in reality, it has given doctors the right to kill. That is why we now see "involuntary euthanasia" and infanticide creeping in, corpse by corpse.

It is sad but ironic that the growing Culture of Death has created a society that is fundamentally suicidal. We have aborted children by their millions, thus eliminating the future taxpayers necessary to fund our healthcare systems. As a result, our healthcare systems bulge with an aging population needing treatment that it will soon be unable to afford. And the Grim Reaper, having wreaked hell and havoc on one end of life's spectrum, materializes at the other end as well. If we cannot afford hospital beds or medicine to treat the elderly and the weak, surely we can afford body bags. All we need then is medical professionals with the discernment to choose who will live and who will die.

The bottom of the slope

Those warning against "assisted suicide" pointed out from the very beginning that so-called "death with dignity" was a lie, carrying with it the not-so-subtle insinuation that for severely ill people to die with dignity, they must die *faster*. But "physician-assisted suicide" became euthanasia-upon-request, and that rapidly became "involuntary euthanasia" and infanticide. We used to call that murder. Facilitating the ending of a life that seemed to have mere hours, days, or weeks left gave way almost immediately to ending lives for virtually any purpose: depression, dementia, blindness, loneliness, disability, autism, and even old age.

Euthanasia advocates, at least for the most part, do not bother to claim they intend to restrict the practice anymore. If we take a brief look at all the places euthanasia regimes have taken root, we see an industry dedicated to streamlining suicide and eugenics. It may not be called eugenics anymore. But everything the eugenicists sought to accomplish: culling the weak, the disabled, the so-called "imperfect" or "defective"—has come creeping back under the guise of "women's rights," "reproductive freedom," the "right to die," and "death with dignity." The voices of those dedicated to suicide prevention, mental health experts, and disability advocates have been tragically ignored.

It is truly chilling to see each and every one of the "slippery slope" warnings made by those opposed to the Culture of Death come to pass, one by one, without a flinch or a blink from those promoting it. The most tangible evidence of deliberate deceit is not simply the fact that the slope did turn out to be slick with blood as many warned, but the fact that those who told us our fears were unfounded and spoke soothingly of "safeguards" and "limitations" accept the corpse-filled trenches at the bottom of said slope with a shrug. In today's culture, all we need to justify more killings is more euphemisms.

Chapter 7

Our Commodity Culture

Evil, I have heard it said, can be defined as treating any human being as an object. If so, the struggle to maintain human exceptionalism as the foundational value of society is properly viewed as existential struggle, if not between good and evil, then certainly between right and wrong.

—Wesley J. Smith, *The Human Exceptionalist*

Never in human history has there been a time in which the buying and selling of human flesh, in one form or another, has been more prevalent. Human trafficking is the fastest growing criminal industry in the world. Pornography depicting the brutalization of women and girls is among the most popular material on the Internet. And abortion, the financed destruction of tiny human beings developing in the womb, claims the lives of almost 42 million pre-born children worldwide each year.

The first time I fully realized how dehumanizing the "sex trade" was, I was a teenager, walking through the streets of Amsterdam with a student group from my school to visit the Church of Our Lord in the Attic, a hidden house church from the 1600s. Our teachers had not realized when they planned the tour, however, that we had to cut directly through the infamous Red Light District in order to get there. As they rushed us down the cobblestone streets with more than a little panic, we gaped at an utterly foreign sight: Rows and rows of windows with scantily clad women standing there, their fatigue painted over with thick layers of makeup and mechanical *come-hither* smiles. *Like meat packages at a butcher shop*, I remember thinking. Even the "souvenir" shops sold only human body parts—postcards featuring only breasts or bottoms, nothing else. It was a human buffet—one brothel owner even compared the tourists viewing the girls to men deciding which pizza to order.

More than 60% of the girls and women who work there report getting sexually assaulted.

The same feeling struck me while traveling in Hungary. My cousin and I arrived in Budapest from Belgrade at four in the morning and climbed into a taxi to find a hostel. The driver soon took us to a less than reputable area of the city in search of an establishment that still had rooms available. I wondered, stupidly, why there were so many young girls still walking about, even though it was dark and the sun was not even stirring. Our taxi pulled up to a stop sign, and I made eye contact with one of them. Her blue eyes were flat and emotionless.

She was very young, and very pretty. She wore a light black jacket with a fur fringe and painted-on pants that must have hurt to walk in. She was freezing—it was so ice-cold that every short breath came out in a puff of steam. An older woman, lounging against an abandoned storefront, barked something at her that I didn't understand, and jerked her head towards me. She started to walk over to the car, gesturing at me and then to herself. That's when I realized that she'd been told to find out if I was a potential customer. I felt quite sick as we drove away, although I was naïve to be so surprised. Budapest, after all, is a sex tourist destination, an Eastern European Bangkok. I'd read about it. I'd just never come face to face with the reality—a girl who should have been in school, selling herself to strangers at the orders of others.

Those who defend legalized prostitution—although the differences between legal and illegal prostitution are few—defend it in much the same way that other horrible practices are defended. "Prostitution advocates often use the word 'choice,'" as Benjamin Nolot of Exodus Cry, an anti-human trafficking organization, noted in his documentary *Nefarious: Merchant of Souls*.

Choice is a sacred word in a culture that worships individualism, and there is no cap on the number of lives that can be sacrificed to it. Joyce Arthur of the Abortion Rights Coalition of Canada, herself a former stripper, occasionally takes time off from promoting abortion to advocate for the legalization of prostitution. "I see a lot of similarity between the issues," she says. "Choice, my body is my own, autonomy, and all those good things."[105]

It should surprise no one that somebody who trumpets the carnage of abortion should also laud an industry that specializes in the degradation of all those who engage with it. After all, this is the same Joyce Arthur who defended Planned Parenthood's dealing in baby parts as a good thing, and even said that Canadian mothers, too, could offer to donate the dismembered body parts of their pre-born children to be used for research. With abortion, as with human trafficking, the pattern is the same: Humans are the sum of their parts, and humans are only valuable in so far as the monetary value of their bodies. Human bodies only serve the purpose of being useful to others.

As I noted in Chapter 4, Dr. Mary Anne Layden, who also researches the links between pornography and human trafficking, put it this way: "This is a business and I think that a lot of pimps would stop doing this if there wasn't any money involved, but it's a business and as soon as you tell somebody it's a product, as soon as you say this [is] something you buy, then this is something you can steal. Those two things are hooked. If you can buy it, you can steal it, and even better if you steal it because then you don't pay for it. So the sexual exploitation industry, whether it's strip clubs or prostitution or pornography, is where you buy it. Sexual violence is where you steal it—rape and child molestation and sexual harassment is where you steal it. So these things are all seamlessly connected. There isn't a way to draw a bright line of demarcation between rape and prostitution and pornography and child molestation. There are not bright lines of demarcation."[106]

When the intentionally sterile sex occasionally results in the production of a child, most pimps and rapists immediately avail themselves of the happy-to-help abortion industry. The mother's body, in their mind, is only useful to serve the sexual needs of paying customers, not to nurture with love and tenderness the tiny, fragile body of her son or daughter. The sexual exploitation industries sell the bodies of women and girls to men, and the abortion industry waits patiently to destroy the unwanted sons and daughters of victims and rapists. Sometimes, they can sell the body parts of those sons and daughters to research firms. All body parts are put to good use. The market gods are happy.

A culture without morals meets capitalism without ethics, and what we have created is a commodity culture. Pornography dehumanizes women for a mass audience, and human trafficking and prostitution allow men to play out their fantasies in real life. When I interviewed anti-sex trafficking activist and then-Member of Parliament Joy Smith, she told me that pimps use today's pornography to groom their victims into accepting assault—and that in studies of johns, huge numbers of them report using prostitution so that they can live out fantasies they would never try on "real women." And the abortionists, of course, can take care of any resulting children, since they are not, in the eyes of our culture, "real children."

Commodity culture, with one trend played out over and over again: Objectification leads to dehumanization. Dehumanization leads to victimization.

Selling life and death

To many readers, the rise of commodity culture will have become ever clearer throughout the preceding chapters. In Chapter 1, I detailed how the Sexual Revolution resulted in sex and the human body being co-opted by the capitalist carpetbaggers who now use sexual imagery to sell every imaginable product. Bodies, it turns out, can also be billboards. It is impossible to walk through a shopping mall without being bombarded by images of near-naked men and women, and clever marketers have attempted to fuse lust and sexual desire with a commercial need to own, *immediately*, whatever they are selling. Instant gratification can take many forms, and our culture has embraced virtually all of them.*

* There is an inherent conflict between the ideology of feminism and the demand for complete, unadulterated sexual liberty. The earlier feminists seemed to recognize this, protesting events that objectified women such as beauty pageants that featured scantily clad women on display for largely male audiences. Feminist intellectuals like Andrea Dworkin condemned pornography in the harshest of terms, as well. Feminists today find themselves rather awkwardly agreeing with Christian condemnations of pornography and the objectification of women, albeit for very different reasons. Some feminists, slowly but surely, are being forced to recognize that the Sexual Revolution has given rise to a commodity culture that poses more of a danger to women than "patriarchy" ever did.

The connections between hook-up culture, the decline of marriage, and abortion have been reviewed comprehensively in Chapters 2 and 5. These connections are more obvious. When sex is extracted from the institution of marriage, the potential for pregnancy becomes a risk rather than an expectation. Even unexpected pregnancies within marriage have the benefit of a context naturally suited to receive children. When sex within hook-up culture is erroneously seen as a matter of "recreation," replacing the traditional recognition of the inherent potential for reproduction, any children resulting from these casual interactions are often seen as an inconvenience, if not an outright hindrance. The abortion industry is more than willing to utilize poisons, forceps, and suction aspirators to rid the parents of these unwanted pests.

To some in our commodity culture, babies in the womb thus have no value as sons or daughters. But as gruesome undercover investigations have revealed, their lifeless bodies do have some value to researchers. Bio-tech firms have been engaged in the business of purchasing the corpses of little girls and little boys for some time now, using them for research and experimentation in the name of medical progress. Fetal and embryonic stem cell research is also a rising trend, with many responding to ethical objections with arguments that boil down to a cold and utilitarian assertion: *Well, they're dead anyway*. Their humanity is ignored, their lives objectified, and their bodies commodified. Objectification, dehumanization, victimization, and finally, commodification.

For others, human life at its earliest stages is commodified in an entirely different way. Parents desperate for children, often and understandably engage in a process known as in vitro fertilization, or IVF. Dr. Robert P. George of Princeton University and Dr. Christopher Tollefsen of the University of South Carolina explain the advent of this procedure in their 2008 book *Embryo: A Defense of Human Life*:

> Some say that the age of embryo technology began on July 25, 1978, with the birth of Louise Brown, the world's first "test tube baby," in England. More accurately, the

> age of embryo technology began nine months earlier, when Louise herself came into existence in a petri dish under the guidance of doctors Patrick Steptoe and Robert Edwards. Since then in vitro fertilization (IVF) has become a significant way of addressing infertility, with nearly 1 percent of all live births in the United States originating in vitro.[107]

This process is not particularly difficult to understand; they write:

> Current IVF techniques are easily understood. In natural human reproduction, a sperm cell from the male penetrates and fertilizes a waiting egg that has been released from the ovary of the mother…The result of successful fertilization is a new single-celled human organism, the zygote…In most cases, of course, the means by which the sperm is introduced into the environment of the egg is sexual intercourse between a man and a woman. But in IVF, the meeting of sperm and egg takes place "in vitro," that is, in a petri dish in a lab (although "in vitro" means "in glass," a petri dish is actually made of plastic.) Typically, the mother-to-be is given drugs to stimulate ovulation. An ultrasound-guided needle is inserted into one of her ovaries and used to retrieve the eggs. Sperm is obtained from the father, and either many sperm are injected into a solution surrounding an egg, or a single sperm is directly inserted into an egg. When the sperm penetrates the egg, the resulting fertilization process takes place just as it would within the mother. After three days, or a bit more, the resulting embryo or embryos are transferred to the mother's uterus. The mother may receive a hormonal treatment to ensure that her uterine lining remains suitable for implantation.[108]

The rise of IVF as a method of addressing infertility starkly highlights how far the commodification of human life has come.* Doctors are paid handsomely to "create" human lives

* Again ironically, some feminists make the same case, arguing that IVF and the resulting phenomenon of surrogate pregnancy, where a woman essentially volunteers to rent her uterus to others and carries their child for them, constitute the commodification of the female body.

in petri dishes and then insert them into the mother. For the newly-created humans, however, IVF is an extraordinarily risky process. In 2010, the American Society for Reproductive Medicine released a report indicating that only 7.5% of all artificially created embryos actually survive long enough to develop and be born alive. Untold thousands of other embryos, unneeded and unheeded by the parents who paid for their creation, remain in freezers for years and often die or are eventually destroyed. Some are sold to research firms. The most fortunate of these abandoned humans are adopted by parents willing to give them a chance at life.*

In one truly gruesome example of how the commodity culture mindset has spread, rising rates of IVF have also resulted in another trend: The plus-one-minus-one pregnancy. As LifeSiteNews reported in 2010:

> David Picella, a Family Nurse Practitioner with specialty training as a medical consultant and teacher of the Creighton Model Fertility Care system, wrote in an article titled "10 Reasons to Choose NaProTechnology Over InVitro Fertilization" that "One of the most objectionable things about IVF is that it can result in a situation where a woman is forced to deal with a dangerously high multiple pregnancy rate.
>
> "Pregnancy risk increases dramatically with the number of babies in the womb. Frequently, women are compelled to selectively 'reduce' (i.e., kill) additional babies in the womb due to unacceptably high pregnancy risk."[109]

This reality has placed some surrogate mothers in an impossibly difficult situation. Surrogacy, in which parents rent the womb of a willing woman in which to gestate their son or daughter, has taken a dark turn as some parents who discover their developing

* While this is still a very controversial issue among Christians, some adoption agencies offer the opportunity to adopt embryos. Nightlight Christian Adoptions, for example, announces on their website that: "Just as each snowflake is frozen, unique and a gift from heaven, so are each of our Snowflake Babies. We hope to help each donated embryo grow, develop and live a full life." They report that 450 babies have already been born as the result of their embryo adoption program.

child is not precisely what they ordered are demanding that surrogate mothers have abortions. The *Washington Post* covered this trend in 2016:

> Brittneyrose Torres, who is about midway through her pregnancy with triplets, told the news media that the biological parents had asked her to "reduce" to minimize medical risks. Her case caught the attention of the Center for Bioethics and Culture Network, a surrogacy watchdog, and her story made national headlines.
>
> Torres told the *New York Post* that she signed a contract for up to $30,000 — $25,000 for one child and an extra $5,000 for more.
>
> She was implanted with two embryos — one that was a female and the other that split into twin males.
>
> She said the couple asked her to eliminate the female, citing medical concerns.
>
> "I emailed my doctors. There were no abnormalities," Torres told the New York Post, referring to a conversation she said she had with the triplets' biological mother. "I told her I couldn't abort one of the children," she added. "I could not emotionally and physically do that at nearly 13 weeks. I believe it will be killing this baby."
>
> Instead, she said, she told them she would be willing to adopt the unwanted child.
>
> Andrew Vorzimer, an attorney for the biological parents and a mediator in the case, said the situation has since been resolved. No lawsuit was ever filed in the case.[110]

Other situations have ended more acrimoniously, with parents offering surrogate mothers thousands of dollars to abort an "imperfect" child or actually suing surrogate mothers who refuse to abort the children they are carrying. Some doctors sell their services creating human life, others sell their services ending human life. Increasingly, human beings brought into this world in a petri dish are at risk of leaving it through the bloody suction hose of an abortionist's aspirator.

In addition to the physicians who sell their services playing God as the givers and takers of human life, other bizarre situations have arisen as the result of the artificial reproduction industry. Men sell their sperm to sperm banks, and this sperm is purchased by those seeking to artificially conceive children.* As the *New York Times* reported in their 2011 investigative report "One sperm donor, 150 offspring," this often has unintended consequences:

> Cynthia Daily and her partner used a sperm donor to conceive a baby seven years ago, and they hoped that one day their son would get to know some of his half siblings—an extended family of sorts for modern times.
>
> So Ms. Daily searched a Web-based registry for other children fathered by the same donor and helped to create an online group to track them. Over the years, she watched the number of children in her son's group grow. And grow.
>
> Today there are 150 children, all conceived with sperm from one donor, in this group of half siblings, and more are on the way. "It's wild when we see them all together—they all look alike," said Ms. Daily, 48, a social worker in the Washington area who sometimes vacations with other families in her son's group.
>
> Now, there is a growing concern among parents, donors and medical experts about potential negative consequences of having so many children fathered by the same donors, including the possibility that genes for rare diseases could be spread more widely through the population. Some experts are even calling attention to the increased odds of accidental incest between half sisters and half brothers, who often live close to one another.

---

* The Center for Bioethics and Culture Network released a documentary called *Anonymous Father's Day* dealing with this topic in 2011.

> "My daughter knows her donor's number for this very reason," said the mother of a teenager conceived via sperm donation in California who asked that her name be withheld to protect her daughter's privacy. "She's been in school with numerous kids who were born through donors. She's had crushes on boys who are donor children. It's become part of sex education" for her.
>
> Critics say that fertility clinics and sperm banks are earning huge profits by allowing too many children to be conceived with sperm from popular donors, and that families should be given more information on the health of donors and the children conceived with their sperm. They are also calling for legal limits on the number of children conceived using the same donor's sperm and a re-examination of the anonymity that cloaks many donors.[111]

It's not just men who are supplying the artificial reproduction industry. Young women are being offered exorbitant amounts of money, sometimes in excess of $100,000 to sell their eggs. Advertisements requesting that women consider this option are cropping up everywhere from university campuses to social media. Many are increasingly critical of this phenomenon, noting that women are rarely informed of the full range of health risks, which ironically include infertility, and that the industry often exploits poor women desperate for money. Many firms specializing in "egg donation" have recently been the target of lawsuits after women found their health adversely impacted by what was supposed to be a simple process. It seems as if harvesting the reproductive capacity of human beings has more consequences than anyone imagined.

Selling sex and death

While the growing market in selling pre-born children may strike many as bizarre, the idea of selling human beings for sex is certainly a more familiar one. Prostitution, after all, is colloquially known as "the world's oldest profession." Dr. Mary Anne Layden refers to prostitution—legal or illegal—along with the porn industry and the various forms of human trafficking as "the sexual exploitation industries." These connections, again, are obvious. A market for purchased sex results in a market for prostitutes, which creates a demand for trafficked humans. In both Canada and the United States, girls and women are trafficked for this purpose—and increasingly, the girls being trafficked are native-born Canadian and American citizens rather than the stereotypical victims from developing countries. To fight this, both the Canadian and American governments have launched initiatives to combat human trafficking: Canada's simply named National Action Plan to Combat Human Trafficking along with the 2005 inclusion of human trafficking as a separate offence in the Criminal Code, and the USA's Victims of Trafficking and Violence Protection Act of 2000.

Pornography does much to drive the market for purchased sex. As then-Member of Parliament Joy Smith told me when Canada's House of Commons was debating a new law on prostitution in 2015, johns often use prostitutes to act out bizarre porn fantasies, many of them cruel and violent. In addition to that, pornography has proven to be a helpful tool for pimps and human traffickers as a method of grooming their victims. With the acts of savagery regularly featured in mainstream porn today, pimps have no problem preparing their victims for what to expect. "I have one victim that I'm giving an award to," Smith told me by phone, "because she's such a courageous person. Her grandfather groomed her with porn and then sold her on the streets. The parents didn't even know what was going on until finally she virtually ran away from home."

When I asked Matt Osborne of Operation Underground Railroad about the connection between porn and human trafficking, he began murmuring in agreement before I could even finish my question. Operation Underground Railroad is a US organization that assists law enforcement officials around the world in breaking up human trafficking rings and rescuing sex slaves, with their operatives going undercover to pose as American sex tourists in shorts and flip-flops to lure human traffickers into revealing their brutal business. Osborne's former employer is the CIA, and he helped work the political transition in Iraq after the fall of Saddam Hussein. Now, he focuses on combatting human trafficking, telling me sombrely that, "If you throw a dart at a globe, wherever it lands, children are being exploited there."

"I've seen it firsthand in a couple of different areas," he said of the connection between porn and human trafficking. "One of the first operations I led in Armenia, Columbia back in October of 2014, we helped take a suspected trafficker in that area who admitted to us...how he got involved in this type of business. He said that when he was 22 years old, he started watching pornography, looking at magazines and videos, and then he just noticed that he needed more and more hard-core, more and more violent pornography to get his fix, so to speak. Then he also realized that he needed to physically have forceful sex with these kids, rape them—he's admitting this to us—and then he actually got in to making pornography. So you see this whole spectrum here—the 'harmless' magazine all the way to having to make pornography. Then some of the American would-be sex buyers we helped to arrest with the Department of Homeland Security, they admitted to us that again, they started with what they thought was harmless pornography and then it got to the point where they actually had to travel to locations to have sex with kids. A couple of them told us, 'I don't think I would be here if it wasn't for pornography.'"

Osborne also pointed out that many of the girls featured in the pornography consumed by North Americans have been trafficked, as well. Not just foreigners, either—former porn star Shelley Lubben says that every girl in the porn industry has been trafficked at one point or another. Even the supposedly happy feminist porn star Belle Knox admitted as much in an interview. "The sex industry has a way of making you very cynical and very bitter," she admitted tiredly. "In a way, I've started to become kind of bitter and a bit cynical. It teaches you to be street smart and not to trust people...I'm so used to being on the lookout for scammers, people who are going to try pimp me out or traffic me. I think my experiences have aged me. I don't have the mind of an eighteen-year-old. I have the emotional baggage of someone much, much older than me."[112]

An industry that provides flesh to consumers online fuels

an industry that sells flesh on street corners, and in brothels, and in dingy hotel rooms. And over and over again, the same cycle: Objectification. Dehumanization. Victimization. Commodification.

How porn fuels abortion

Porn culture fuels abortion culture as well, and this has a profound impact on the pro-life movement. Pornography and abortion are both inherently dehumanizing. Abortion ideology reduces pre-born children to disposable objects. Porn ideology reduces women to sex object status. If men dehumanize the women they see, it's that much easier for them to dehumanize the child they can't see.

Especially when talking to high school students, the impact of porn use is becoming more readily apparent. It's not hard to see why: If over 80% of men are systematically dehumanizing women and girls through the use of pornography, it's that much more difficult to convince them that the pre-born are human, too. Most of them haven't even given children in the womb much thought—as I mentioned previously, they've already separated sex from pregnancy.

When we pro-life activists engage these students—the first boys and girls of the Porn Generation—the task of convincing them of the pro-life view can be more difficult than simply illustrating scientifically the humanity of the pre-born child to them. We must combat both abortion ideology as well as porn ideology, and fight dehumanization on two fronts. With many people, I have found that appealing to the role of men in standing up for the women in their lives and protecting their children is very effective. However, porn ideology is attacking the very role of men and everything good and noble about masculinity. In short, many boys no longer have any idea about what it means to be a man. The idea that men should *protect* women and children runs contrary to everything they consume online.

Any pro-life activist can attest to the fact that female pro-life activists are often subjected to stomach-churning verbal abuse. My female colleagues have, in my hearing, been told they should be raped, told they are vile and ugly (they're all quite beautiful, for the record), and called names that, I discovered in my research, find their origins in pornography. Pro-life activists from every part of the movement can attest to similar abuse. The shocking prevalence of the "c-word" is a direct result of porn ideology. Dr. Gail Dines refers to mainstream pornography as "hate speech against women." In that vein, I think it's fair to say that the "c-word" is to misogyny what the "n-word" is to racism. The verbal abuse men subject women to in public today would have been unthinkable mere decades ago. Chivalry isn't just dead, it's been butchered.

Porn also robs the pro-life movement of men. It's always a bit amusing to me when people say the pro-life movement is made up of old men. In fact, most pro-life organizations are made up primarily of women rather than men. I've found, time and time again, that the reason for this is the fact that huge numbers of Christian and pro-life men struggle with pornography. Many of them are convicted by the abortion issue, and many of them are truly passionate about helping their neighbors. But the guilt and shame from porn addiction cripples and castrates them, and when they confront themselves with the hypocrisy of standing up for women and children in public while participating in the dehumanization and victimization of women through pornography in private, they often choose to not get involved. The pro-life movement—and I would wager many other worthy causes—are thus robbed of many talented and passionate men by the scourge of pornography. The porn industry has successfully turned customers into collaborators in the commodity culture.

Our soulless future

Commodity culture exists because our materialist society no longer believes in the existence of the soul. They've forgotten that we have both a body and a soul. Yet, it is the soul that comes up time and time again when those who have been involved in the exploitation industries struggle to explain the depth and brutality of the damage that has been done. "Every time I sold myself, I felt like I was selling my soul," said one former prostitute. No one understands "the pain and destruction to a woman's heart and soul" that is inflicted by the sex trade, explained Annie Lobert, a former sex worker. When he brought young women onto the porn sets, "I watched their souls die," one former porn producer told me.

Again and again, former victims and former perpetrators struggle to find words to describe the destruction our commodity culture has wrought, and time and time again they find themselves drawn to words that beckon towards the transcendent. They know, because they have felt the pain and the horror, that human beings are not simply two randomly-ordered bodies of flesh that can come together for brief physical pleasure. We are so much more than that. We were not built for abuse and degradation, but for love and dignity.

Many times throughout the history of humanity, we have forgotten these simple truths. And that is why, more than two hundred years after the great Christian abolitionist William Wilberforce triumphed in his battle against the slave trade, we are again fighting the same evils. We tossed out God and truth, and the pimps and flesh-peddlers came creeping back in. We announced that humans were simply animals, and human traffickers and pornographers obligingly treated them as such. We taught everyone that materialism explained everything and that souls did not exist—and the abortionists nodded and busied their tools to begin the work of dismembering and discarding the soulless clumps of cells we once recognized as our perfectly created sons and daughters.

Things have never been perfect. Prostitution and infanticide are as old as time. But we once collectively recognized these things as awful practices that preyed on the most vulnerable, and sought to stamp them out. Now, we live in a culture that has abandoned the moral framework necessary to recognize transcendent concepts like the dignity of the human person, the sanctity of human life, and infinite preciousness of the human soul.

It is when we begin to recognize these things that, through the human rubble and sex-driven carnage, we can again turn to a place where we realize that the value of a human being cannot be monetized, and that to try such a thing is an evil that spawns unstoppable wickedness.

Chapter 8

Who Killed Religious Freedom?

Moral revolutions require legal revolutions. This is certainly the case with the sexual revolution and its various causes of sexual liberation. A revolution is only complete when the legal structure aligns itself with a new moral understanding. This alignment is exactly what is taking place in American public life on the issue of gay liberation. Every society has a structure of systems that either influences or coerces behavior. Eventually, societies move to legislate and regulate behavior in order to align the society with what is commonly, or at least largely, considered morally right and wrong.

—R. Albert Mohler, Jr., *We Cannot Be Silent*

What we are experiencing in Canada and the United States is not simply a moral revolution. It is a moral *reversal*. It is not simply that the majority of people *disagree* with Christian values. It is that the majority of people genuinely find Christian values *morally repugnant*. Not only have the Christian values that formed the civilizational foundation of our respective countries been tossed away, they have been replaced by other values. Unfettered sexual liberty, no-fault divorce, pornography, abortion, euthanasia—these are no longer put forward as necessary evils, but as social boons. "Woe unto them," the prophet Isaiah once warned, "that call evil good, and good evil; that put darkness for light, and light for darkness; that put bitter for sweet, and sweet for bitter!"

While not all legal cases against Christians have been successful and some have even been overturned, the tide of legal opinion is now flowing definitively against us. In 2002, for example, the

Supreme Court of Ontario, Canada, forced a Catholic school in Whitby to permit a male student to bring his boyfriend to prom.

In 2003, a so-called Human Rights Tribunal in British Columbia ordered the Knights of Columbus, a Catholic men's organization, to pay a lesbian couple $2,000 in "damages" for declining to rent their hall for a same-sex wedding. The ruling actually cited "injury…to their feelings."

Later that same year, a teacher was given a professional misconduct citation by the British Columbia College of Teachers for writing a letter to the editor of a local newspaper that described the Christian view of homosexual behavior. Regardless of the fact that this letter was written on his own time and as a private citizen, Chris Kempling's actions were considered to be misconduct and he was duly disciplined.

In 2007, an Alberta Human Rights Commission demanded that Christian pastor Stephen Boisson publicly apologize for a column he wrote in a local newspaper outlining his opposition to the gay liberation movement.*

An Oregon judge fined a Christian couple who ran a bakery $135,000 for declining to bake a wedding cake for a lesbian couple in 2013. Gay activists launched a campaign of harassment against Aaron and Melissa Klein, and they were forced to shut down their bakery.

That same year, the Attorney General of Washington State launched a lawsuit against Arlene's Flowers when the florist declined to provide flowers for a gay wedding celebration.

In 2015, Colorado baker Jack Phillips of Masterpiece Cakeshop had to stop making wedding cakes altogether after Colorado courts ruled that he could not refuse to assist gay wedding celebrations.

---

* In 2009 after being forced to appear before the Alberta Human Rights Tribunal himself, conservative commentator Ezra Levant published a book titled *Shakedown: How Our Government is Undermining Democracy in the Name of Human Rights*, detailing the flagrant abuses and totalitarian actions of so-called human rights tribunals across Canada.

And on and on it goes. As our society's governments and legal apparatuses realign with the new morality, stunned Christians are finding themselves in the crosshairs. Christian universities find their lifestyle policies under attack and are accused of being discriminatory. Christian bakeries, florists, and property owners who do not wish to participate in gay wedding celebrations are finding themselves persecuted not just by gay rights activists, but by their own government. Christian charities are sidelined due to their beliefs, and adoptive and foster parents fear that they will be passed over due to their now-bigoted beliefs.

Even when Christians succeed in defending their religious liberty in the courts, the public backlash is fierce. One example of this is the Hobby Lobby case, where a Christian-owned arts and craft store took the U.S. government to court over President Barack Obama's national healthcare plan in 2014:

> The court ruled that Hobby Lobby and Conestoga Wood Specialties, privately held companies founded and managed by Christian families, had a religious liberty to refuse coverage for drugs that might function as abortifacients in their health care plans for employees. More than the case itself, the reaction to the court's decision is both illuminating and deeply concerning. The secular culture has responded with outright alarm and indignation that the court would rule that these two companies have the right to defy the prevailing wisdom of the contraception movement and the government's efforts to coerce their participation.[113]

As Christian churches and institutions, to say nothing of leaders and laypeople, try to understand what is taking place and how we are to respond, it is again important that we recognize what has unfolded during the decades since the Sexual Revolution. Triumphalism is beginning to seep into the psyche of the revolutionaries, and the erosion and eradication of religious liberty we see taking place is the end game of the most successful revolutions in human history.

An overnight transformation?

On Election Night 2004, I commented to a friend that things were not nearly so bad as the doomsayers liked to claim. George W. Bush won both the election and the popular vote, after all, and he had advocated an amendment to the U.S. Constitution that would affirm that marriage was between one man and one woman. Eleven states passed amendments banning gay marriage with huge majorities. But as Albert Mohler notes, "In retrospect, the 2004 votes were the last gasp of the defense of marriage in a culture trending secular."[114]

A few short years later, the fault lines over gay marriage were spreading even into the conservative movement. In 2010, Focus on the Family threatened to pull its sponsorship of the Conservative Political Action Conference (CPAC), the nation's largest annual gathering of the conservative movement, over the fact that the gay Republican group GOProud would be co-sponsoring. GOProud was a fierce supporter of gay marriage, and their presence at CPAC was felt. When conservative writer Ryan Sorba articulated the case for natural law at the conference, he was booed long and loud. I sat in the audience, stunned. The libertarian friend I'd attended with grimaced awkwardly. Things were obviously changing fast when someone could get booed for articulating facts that virtually everyone once took for granted a few short years ago at the *most conservative conference in America*. A mere three years later, I was in the crowd in front of the Capitol as Barack Obama changed his tune on gay marriage in his Second Inaugural Address. "Our journey is not complete until our gay brothers and sisters are treated like anyone else under the law," he thundered, "for if we are truly created equal, then surely the love we commit to one another must be equal as well!" Two years later, in 2015, Obama had the White House lit up in rainbow colors to celebrate the U.S. Supreme Court's imposition of gay marriage on all fifty states.

This shift seemed sudden to many Christians, but only because most were not watching carefully. As with so many other aspects of the Sexual Revolution, the gay agenda was plotted out far in advance by activists who laid out much of their strategy. In the 1989 book *After the Ball: How America Will Conquer Its Fear and Hatred of Gays in the 90's,* Marshall Kirk and Hunter Madsen detailed, step by step, how important it was to ensure that society began to see homosexuals as victims in order to translate the resulting human empathy into sympathy for the political goals of the gay liberation movement. The AIDS crisis, which first began to devastate the gay community in San Francisco and New York in the early 1980s, fit the bill perfectly. Kirk and Madsen were willing to admit that their refusal to waste this crisis would appear as crass opportunism, writing that, "As cynical as it seems, AIDS gives us a chance, however brief, to establish ourselves as a victimized minority legitimately deserving of America's protection and care."[115]

When victims could not be found, the gay liberation movement invented them.[*] The most prominent example of this was the murder of Matthew Shepard in 1998. The twenty-two-year-old University of Wyoming student was brutally beaten and left to die sometime during the night of October 6, and his killing was trumpeted by gay rights activists as evidence of the brutality that gays and lesbians experienced as a matter of course. They demanded that federal hate crime legislation be expanded to include the gay community, and Barack Obama signed The Matthew Shepard and James Byrd Jr. Hate Crimes Prevention Act into law in 2009.[**] However, a 2013 book by gay author Stephen Jimenez called *The Book of Matt: The Truth About the Murder of Matthew Shepard* told a much different story. Jimenez,

* Social conservative news outlets such as LifeSiteNews.com regularly publish exposes of fictitious hate crimes against members of the gay community, many of them invented for the sole purpose of claiming victimhood status and demonizing opponents of the Sexual Revolution.

** James Byrd Jr. was an African American man savagely murdered by three men in Texas in 1998, at least two of which were white supremacists. The name of the bill itself reveals one of the gay liberation movement's most effective strategies: claiming that they are the moral descendants of the African-American struggle for civil rights, in effect comparing opposition to gay marriage and other gay "rights" with segregation and racism and implying that sexual preference or orientation is as immutable as race. The fact that the Rev. Martin Luther King Jr., the Baptist pastor who led the Civil Rights Movement until his assassination in 1968, held to the orthodox Christian position on homosexuality and wrote as much in a 1958 advice column in *Ebony Magazine*, simply reveals the extent to which the gay liberation movement has successfully managed to distort history.

no foe of the gay rights cause, lays out in convincing evidence that Shepard was not murdered for being gay, but that the killing was the result of a drug deal gone bad. Shepard, it turns out, was a meth dealer who actually knew his murderers. This book was largely ignored by the mainstream press. The truth didn't fit the narrative. Besides, Matthew Shepard, Gay Rights Martyr, had already served his purpose.

Playing the victim worked. Ted Byfield's history *The High Tide and the Turn* detailed the rainbow blitzkrieg:

> All through the 1980s and into the 1990s, the AIDS juggernaut advanced, as did the gay-rights movement. 'Gay pride' parades across America each June grew larger, more ubiquitous, and more indecent. In major cities they became almost orgiastic displays of public nudity, garish costumes, and lewd gestures, although this did not dissuade prominent political and community figures from leading them. Police departments established gay liaison task forces to combat hate crimes, and high schools, far from educating youth about the hazardous reality of homosexual practice, instead condoned and promoted it by opening "gay-straight" student clubs under the guise of anti-bullying initiatives.[116]

In order to portray homosexuals as victims, the gay liberation movement needed *victimizers*, as well. Just as Dr. Bernard Nathanson and his co-conspirators in the abortion movement had successfully scapegoated the Catholic hierarchy as the murderers of women who died during back-alley abortions, the gay liberation movement decided to emulate this strategy and demonize Christian opponents as the de-facto killers of gay youth. This would take a clever propaganda campaign, designed to rob Christian churches of their traditional image as benefactors of the poor and downtrodden and transform them into ugly persecutors of society's most disenfranchised members. Kirk and Madsen described how this could be achieved:

> For example, for several seconds an unctuous, beady-eyed Southern preacher is shown pounding the pulpit in rage against "those perverted, abominable creatures."

> While his tirade continues over the soundtrack, the picture switches to heart-rending photos of badly beaten persons, or of gays who look decent, harmless, and likeable; and then we cut back to the poisonous face of the preacher. The contrast speaks for itself. The effect will be devastating.[117]

And indeed it was. Christians in the twenty-first century often express bewilderment at the anger and vitriol directed towards them and their beliefs, and the reality is that Christians were the victims of a superbly thought-out propaganda campaign that did not simply seek to humanize gay and lesbian people, but to *dehumanize* all those who disagreed with the agenda of the gay liberation movement.

With a little help from the churches

It is essential to note here the insidious danger of hypocrisy and inconsistency within the Christian community, especially now. When *genuine* hatred of those who suffer from same-sex attraction surfaces in churches—and it would be deceitful to claim that it is completely nonexistent—it almost immediately results in a media firestorm. Such incidents, even though they are aberrations, confirm the caricatures the gay liberation movement has been carefully creating for decades. It is not unfair to say that the repulsive antics of the Westboro Baptist Church have done more to further the cause of gay liberation than any drag queen prancing down the street during a Pride Parade ever has.*

It is impossible to underestimate how effective the campaign to whip up hatred and contempt for Christian beliefs and Christian people has been. The dehumanization has worked particularly well, with Christians now routinely referred to as "bigots," "homophobes," and other recently-invented epithets by media

---

* The Westboro Baptist Church is a tiny protest organization made up almost completely of the extended family of the late Fred Phelps. They travel the United States protesting military funerals and other solemn occasions, waving signs containing slogans such as "God Hates Fags." Their efforts have served most notably in providing fodder for those in the media seeking to paint Christian churches as universally "homophobic," and stock photos of Westboro Baptist protests are routinely used to accompany media articles detailing Christian opposition to gay marriage.

organizations that have long abandoned any pretence of neutrality. I recall vividly one conversation with a man I worked with extensively during my time at university, on a number of campaigns designed to combat anti-Semitism. He was gay, and had a long-time male partner. The prevalence of various gay rights campaigns in the media led to many fascinating conversations between the two of us, in which I detailed the Christian position on gay marriage. All of these exchanges remained courteous and amicable. Several years later, after the U.S. Supreme Court had legalized gay marriage, I was chatting with him about rising rates of anti-Semitism on campus in Canada, and he remarked, off-handedly, that "homophobic" opposition to gay marriage was dissipating, so perhaps anti-Semitism would, too. "Would you call me a homophobe?" I asked him, knowing that he was fully aware of my position. He paused, and swallowed uncomfortably. "I suppose I'd just call you a friend," he replied, and changed the subject. It is harder for gay rights advocates to dehumanize their opponents, it seems, when they are faced with actual people who seek to articulate the truth of the Christian position rather than confirm the caricature.*

Some Christian denominations also found themselves ill-equipped to respond to the challenges of the gay liberation movement because they had already accepted many of the premises of the Sexual Revolution in the first place. Many churches accepted no-fault divorce and ignored rising divorce rates within their own congregations. Contraception was accepted by enormous numbers of lay Catholics, and most Protestant churches mounted no theological objection to the use of contraceptives as a means of family planning. In fact, very few Protestants even remember the fact that opposition to contraception had been a universally accepted Christian dogma across all denominational lines until 1930, when the Anglican Church first decided to permit the limited use of birth control.** Having accepted the presence of

* My colleagues and I in the pro-life movement have found the same thing to be true over and over again in conversations about abortion. Those holding to a pro-abortion position are consistently surprised when they engage with pro-lifers who do not shout, scream, or say hateful things, and many are forced to admit that the media stereotype of the pro-life movement is false.

** It's worth noting that the birth control pill is now widely condemned by pro-life apologists due to its potentially abortifacient qualities.

cultural trends which severely undermined marriage as a life-long commitment and the once intrinsic connection between marriage and child-bearing, many Christian leaders found themselves effectively disarmed of many essential apologetics concerning the true nature of sexuality and marriage.

Liberal churches, on the other hand, served as convenient collaborators for the gay liberation movement. Just as the abortion activists in both Canada and the United States had targeted pseudo-Christian churches that had long repudiated anything resembling orthodoxy to gain support for their abortion-legalization campaigns, Kirk and Madsen detailed how the support of churches was essential for their campaigns, as well. If the gay liberation activists could convince liberal denominations to support their cause and erode the resolve of weak-kneed churches through massive cultural pressure, they could utilize such endorsements to claim moral legitimacy for their cause.

As liberal churches began to permit same-sex relationships, take steps towards the ordination of gay clergy, and make approving noises concerning gay marriage, gay activists were able to send a loud message to a culture that was awaiting the Christian response. They could effectively push to the fringe orthodox Christian denominations who held to 2,000 years of Christian teaching on sexuality, while declaring that the liberal denominations—(those who endorse *love in all its forms*)—were the true representatives of Christianity in the West. That is why orthodox Christians who despise homophobia have found themselves consistently lumped in with the hatemongering Westboro Baptists—because the gay liberation movement has, through the careful cultivation of alliances with post-Christian churches, redefined for many in the culture at large what it means to be a Christian. Adhering to orthodoxy is no longer important, they say. Not judging the actions of your neighbors, however, is paramount: Judge not, except when you are judging those you find judgemental.

A mask of normality

It was also important, Kirk and Madsen wrote, to ensure that average citizens were made to see homosexuals as people no different from them. "When we say *talk* about homosexuality," they emphasized, "we mean just that. In the early stages of the campaign, the public should not be shocked and repelled by premature exposure to homo*sexual* behavior itself.* Instead, the imagery of sex per se should be downplayed, and the issue of gay rights reduced, as far as possible, to an abstract social question."[118]

It was this sort of attitude—the fear that exposure to the reality of the gay lifestyle would turn off potential supporters of the movement's political goals--that was on display in a satire column published in *The Onion* in 2001 titled "Gay-Pride Parade Sets Mainstream Acceptance Of Gays Back 50 Years:"

> The mainstream acceptance of gays and lesbians, a hard-won civil-rights victory gained through decades of struggle against prejudice and discrimination, was set back at least 50 years Saturday in the wake of the annual Los Angeles Gay Pride Parade.
>
> "I'd always thought gays were regular people, just like you and me, and that the stereotype of homosexuals as hedonistic, sex-crazed deviants was just a destructive myth," said mother of four Hannah Jarrett, 41, mortified at the sight of 17 tanned and oiled boys cavorting in jock straps to a throbbing techno beat on a float shaped like an enormous phallus. "Boy, oh, boy, was I wrong."
>
> The parade, organized by the Los Angeles Gay And Lesbian And Bisexual And Transvestite And Transgender Alliance (LAGALABATATA), was intended to "promote acceptance, tolerance, and equality for the city's gay community." Just the opposite, however, was accomplished, as the event confirmed the worst fears of

* The gay liberation movement itself was divided in terms of tactics. While it was generally agreed upon that strategies like those of Kirk and Madsen would work most effectively, the radical wing of the movement somewhat scornfully referred to these activists as "assimilationists." As far as they were concerned, marriage was an archaic and restrictive institution, monogamy was suffocating in practice, and they had no desire to be seen by anyone as "normal." They did not want to convince the public that they were "just like them," because they were not and they didn't want to be. It was these "liberationists" that often made up the more exhibitionist aspects of the Gay Pride parades.

> thousands of non-gay spectators, cementing in their minds a debauched and distorted image of gay life straight out of the most virulent right-wing hate literature.[119]

The task of normalizing homosexual behavior was made much easier by the Sexual Revolution that had already transformed the way the majority of North Americans felt about sex and had conveniently eliminated many of the moral boundaries that had once existed. Gay activists found themselves pushing against an open door. The gay liberation movement sought to present themselves as "normal," but Alfred Kinsey had already successfully smashed the idea that "normal" existed in the first place. The movement was selective in its presentation of Kinsey's work: Kirk and Madsen explained that the average person had to be convinced that homosexuality consisted of fixed orientations incapable of shift or evolution, that gays and lesbians were "born that way." Thus, those who opposed homosexual behavior could be presented as hateful bigots who discriminated against homosexuals based on *who they were*. To oppose homosexual behavior, they posited, was no different than hating homosexuals themselves.

Leaving aside the fact that the reality of sexual attraction is far more complicated, these assertions did not even align with Alfred Kinsey's infamous "Kinsey Scale," which presented sexuality as completely fluid and claimed that a person could fall anywhere on a scale of 0 to 6, with 0 meaning the person was exclusively heterosexual and 6 meaning the person was exclusively homosexual. Although the idea of sexuality (and gender) being completely fluid has now been embraced by the LGBTQ movement, it was initially ignored by many as politically problematic. The idea that sexual attraction could change was inconvenient to their goals and contradicted their claim that homosexuals were a group worthy of special legal recognition and protection.* In 1973, a raucous and effective

* In fact, researchers are just beginning to discover that sexual attractions can be impacted by a variety of factors, not the least of which is the compulsive use of pornography. In his 2007 book *The Brain That Changes Itself: Stories of Personal Triumph from the Frontiers of Brain Science*, psychiatrist Norman Doidge examines how porn can distort and transform sexual urges and desires.

campaign by gay activists resulted in the American Psychiatric Association declassifying homosexuality as a disorder, and the American Psychological Association followed suit in 1975. The World Health Organization held out until 1990—by then, to disagree with same-sex attraction on mental health grounds was already considered heresy by the medical establishment.*

The gay liberation movement had (and has) no stronger ally than the entertainment industry. From the boundary-smashing, drug-fuelled anthems to hedonism that shrieked to the top of the music charts to Hollywood films and TV shows increasingly bent on showcasing with approval alternative sexual lifestyles, everyday men and women face a non-stop barrage of cleverly crafted propaganda. It is now virtually impossible to find any television show that does not feature gay characters, and Hollywood films lionizing figures of the gay rights movement or presenting gay relationships as virtually identical to heterosexual relationships are common. The smash-hit '90s sitcom *Friends*, for example, featured one of the very first mainstream representations of a gay wedding in 1996, portraying a lesbian relationship (one that had broken up a marriage) tenderly while presenting parents who disapproved of the same-sex wedding as ugly bigots. The show's producers admitted that they had expected huge backlash, and were shocked when there was very little response at all. Rather than the thousands of angry phone calls NBC expected to receive, they instead received only four.

It is partially because gay characters are so predominant in entertainment that many people believe homosexuality is far more prevalent than it actually is. According to a 2015 Gallup Poll, the American public believes that 23% of the population is gay or lesbian. In reality, only 3.8% of Americans identify as gay, lesbian, bi-sexual, or transgender.[120] Canadian numbers are similar.** This explains why issues presumably impacting only a tiny number of people—which bathroom a transgender person uses, for example—end up commanding so much attention. The LGBTQ movement

---

* Jeffrey Satinover, a Jewish psychiatrist, details the successful campaign of the gay rights activists in his 1996 book *Homosexuality and the Politics of Truth.*

** The oft-repeated claim that an average of 10% of people are homosexual originates in Dr. Alfred Kinsey's junk science.

has effectively infiltrated and recruited the entertainment industry and the mainstream media, and are successfully using these avenues to change how the culture perceives homosexuality and the political goals of their movement.

In spite of all of this, the gay liberation movement is not satisfied with their progress and is not finished their campaign to root out dissent and demand compulsory acceptance of their lifestyles. In fact, the Gay and Lesbian Alliance Against Defamation (GLAAD) actually claims that they are *underrepresented* in Hollywood, specifically condemning Disney for not including gay characters in their animated films. "According to GLAAD's fourth annual studio report card," the news website Collider.com reported, "which grades Hollywood studios on how well they included LGBT characters in their films, not one studio received a marking of 'Good.' Out of the 126 films released in 2015, only 22 (which amounts to 17.5%) included LGBT characters, the same percentage recorded in 2014. Lionsgate, Sony, Universal, and Fox received 'Adequate' ratings, but Warner Bros., Paramount, and Disney all earned 'Failing.'" Gay activists do not simply want to be proportionately represented by the entertainment industry, they want to be *predominantly* represented.[121] One telling example is the fact that *Friends*, the TV show that worked hard to mainstream homosexuality, is now not gay enough for gay rights activists, who have taken to the pages of publications such as Slate.com and *Cosmopolitan* to decry the "homophobia" that can apparently be found in many of the sitcom's jokes.

Law is downstream from culture, and the menacing undercurrents of totalitarianism that Christian intellectuals always warned were present in the gay rights movement are beginning to manifest themselves. Some of its victims are stunned to find out that they possess some sort of phobia.* Radical feminist Germaine Greer,

* Laws are also powerful as educational tools. In a time where increasing numbers of people have no moral framework for what is right and what is wrong, many defer to the law as the final arbiter of morality. Pro-life activists presenting the case that abortion is wrong often receive the response: "But it's legal!" The legalization of same-sex marriage and the realignment of our legal systems in favor of same-sex relationships has thus had the effect of cementing the cultural conception in the minds of many that same-sex marriage is not only permissible, but good and just. Opposition to same-sex marriage, it then follows, must be wicked and unjust.

for example, found herself loudly denounced by gay activists for condemning the idea that transgender men could understand the female experience, an assertion she found understandably offensive. When Mozilla CEO Brendan Eich was forced to step down from his position in 2014 for a donation he'd made to a campaign to protect natural marriage nearly a decade earlier, atheist and gay rights supporter Bill Maher commented on his HBO TV show that he thought "there is a gay mafia. I think if you cross them, you get wacked."* Gay culture warriors have been incredibly effective—as Scottish politician Andrew Fletcher once noted, "Give me the makings of a people's songs, and I care not who makes its laws." Politicians, after all, inevitably march to the tune they hear.

There is one rarely-discussed cultural current that has done much to normalize homosexual behavior: Pornography. Pornography has destroyed our ability to be shocked or scandalized, and has been instrumental in eliminating any stigma surrounding alternative sexual lifestyles. If over 80% of men and close to half of women are viewing pornography every single month, how can we possibly expect them to be shocked by the exhibitionism and lewdness of the Gay Pride Parade? Within the confines of our homes we are watching thousands upon thousands of naked people committing every sex act imaginable, over and over again, day after day. When we emerge blinking into the sun, should it be any surprise that parades prominently featuring public nudity and bizarre sexuality do not ruffle us in the least? For many, it's just as if the scenes they devour on the screens of their laptops and television sets have leaked onto the street. The once-shocking displays of nudity and sexuality on the streets of our cities are now positively tame compared to the pornographic entertainment enjoyed in private by much of the public.

---

* Eich had donated to the 2008 Proposition 8 campaign, which saw voters in California reject a court decision legalizing gay marriage. This campaign was detailed extensively in the pro-gay documentary *8: The Mormon Proposition*, in which a number of journalists and gay rights activists rejected Christian concerns that same-sex marriage threatened religious freedom as viciously and intentionally deceitful. It's worth noting that since same-sex marriage was established in California, every single concern put forward by Christians has been unfortunately validated.

Pornography is also the reason that so many young evangelicals and Catholics are flocking to join the ranks of those calling for the redefinition of marriage. After all, anal sex and a buffet of other sex acts are mainstream in pornography. Can anyone expect those raised on this sexual diet to mount any protest against those calling for the state to formalize and endorse "alternative" sexual relationships? Especially when in droves, young Christians are beginning to experiment with alternative sexual lifestyles themselves? Gay rights activist and writer Andrew Sullivan pointed this out with glee in his essay, "We are all sodomites now: a case for sexual freedom," in which he pointed out that since heterosexual couples were overwhelmingly engaging in sexual activity that Christian teaching once condemned as "sodomy," moral objections to sodomy within a same-sex relationship had no grounding. By their own behaviors, Sullivan points out (not incorrectly) that the inconsistency of today's Christians has effectively eliminated much of their credibility on such matters.

Pornography has successfully normalized virtually every sex act, and as the result, they have become normal. *The Telegraph* reported on this trend some time ago:

> According to a new piece of research by two American university professors, the more porn heterosexual men watch – the more it opens up their mind to be increasingly accepting of "non-traditional sexual situations".
>
> "Our study suggests that the more heterosexual men, especially less educated heterosexual men, watch pornography, the more supportive they become of same-sex marriage," Indiana University Assistant Professor Paul Wright told The Washington Examiner.
>
> "Pornography adopts an individualistic, non-judgmental stance on all kinds of non-traditional sexual behaviours and same-sex marriage attitudes are strongly linked to attitudes about same-sex sex.
>
> "If people think individuals should be able to decide for themselves whether to have same-sex sex, they will

> also think that individuals should be able to decide for themselves whether to get married to a partner of the same-sex."[122]

The normalization of homosexuality is now complete. Many liberal churches openly endorse and celebrate same-sex relationships, and other religious quislings are sure to follow in droves as cultural pressure increases. The entertainment industry showcases same-sex relationships, and the mainstream media promotes the political goals of the gay liberation movement. Corporations are responding to the new cultural consensus by scrambling to wrap themselves in the rainbow flag, and conservative and libertarian politicians are rooting around for ways to do the same without losing the votes of their Christian constituents. Christian communities, meanwhile, have been so poisoned by pornography that many voices which should have been lifted in dissent were reduced to silence by the shame of hypocrisy, and the rapidly changing views of many young congregants find their roots in the filth their minds have been clogged with since adolescence.*

Kirk and Madsen's strategy has worked.

The New Normal Versus the Old Morals

The rejection of natural marriage and the traditional family structure is creating conflict on a thousand fronts.** Gay couples, for example, cannot conceive children naturally and are thus demanding that they be allowed to adopt children. Christian adoption agencies are finding themselves forced into untenable situations, and some have considered closing their doors altogether. Commodity culture, of course, is somewhat able to satisfy the gay community's demand for children—with artificial insemination, surrogacy, and in vitro fertilization, human beings can always be made to order and handed over to

---

* One recent poll indicated that up to half of evangelical pastors admitted to viewing pornography in the past year.

** One of the best books to come out on the definition of marriage is *What is Marriage? Man and Woman: A Defense*, by Sherif Gergis, Ryan T. Anderson, and Robert P. George.

their buyers to create facsimile families.*

In both the United States and Canada, the state is intervening on the side of the Sexual Revolution and the gay liberation movement to force collaboration, complicity, and approval. For decades, gay activists claimed that they had no beef with religious liberty, and that same-sex marriage would never impact the freedoms of conscientious objectors. Scarcely were their political goals achieved before they began to reject the concept of religious liberty out of hand, refusing to recognize it as a legitimate concept altogether. Left-wing news sites regularly run stories "debunking" the idea of religious liberty. As Albert Mohler wrote, "The conflict of liberties means that the new moral regime, with the backing of the courts and the regulatory state, will prioritize erotic liberty over religious liberty."[123]

While gay activists are rejecting religious liberty openly and brazenly by launching campaigns against bakers, photographers, and property owners who respectfully decline to assist them in celebrating their relationships, politicians are attempting to undermine religious liberty more subtly. As Mohler noted:

> Even while religious liberty is supposedly being recognized and affirmed, it is often being transformed and minimized. The Obama administration provides a classic example of this. Numerous representatives of the administration, including President Obama himself, have shifted their language from "freedom of religion" to "freedom of worship." Though these two phrases may appear to be very similar, freedom of worship is a severe and deadly reduction of freedom of religion. Religious freedom is not limited to what takes place within the confines of a church building and its worship. Freedom of worship marginalizes and ghettoizes Christian speech so that its liberties only exist within the confines

* This is far more radical than many might think. When governments approve adoptions by gay couples, they are making a very clear statement: Either the father or the mother are unnecessary for the well-being of a child. Those of different sexes are the same, and bring nothing unique to the table in the family context.

> of a church facility—but it does not guarantee a right to public voice. Freedom of worship essentially muzzles the Christian in the public square.[124]

Those gay activists who attempt to defend religious liberty are promptly marginalized. The writer and commentator Andrew Sullivan, for example, has found himself unwelcome on many campuses because even though he campaigned for same-sex marriage for years, he believes the gay liberation movement must respect religious liberty. When he defended Brendan Eich over his Proposition 8 donation, he faced enormous backlash. Jonathan Rauch, another campaigner for same-sex marriage, has also attempted to rebuke his fellow activists in his book *Kindly Inquisitors: The New Attacks on Free Thought*. He too, is ignored. The lightning speed with which gay activists have abandoned their commitment to leave Christians in peace has earned the nickname "The Law of Merited Impossibility: It will never happen, and when it does, you bigots deserve it."[125]

Immediately following on the heels of the same-sex marriage victories, LGBTQ activists moved from redefining reality to abolishing it altogether. The ongoing "bathroom wars" and fights over biological men and women who identify as the opposite sex have bewildered many people, as they seem to have repudiated common sense altogether. In essence, a man possessing a perfectly functioning set of male genitalia should, according to the LGBTQ movement, be permitted access to the women's bathroom based on his assertion that he is a female. People should be permitted to choose their gender, or be recognized based on their perception of reality rather than reality as it actually is. As Mohler writes:

> The transgender revolution is so new on the scene that most Americans are not even certain how to talk about it...The pioneers of the transgender revolution were identified as transvestites, which linguistically referred mostly to clothing and "cross-dressing." Those changing their gender by totally immersing themselves in the gender opposite from their biological sex were called transsexuals. Today, a transsexual may or may

> not have had gender reassignment surgery or hormonal treatments, but a very clear declaration to be identified as the opposite gender has been made. Transgender means exactly what it appears to mean—moving through and beyond the category of gender as it has been defined in the past. It alone reveals the comprehensiveness of this revolution.[126]

The end result of this revolution is to establish a new moral order in which, to paraphrase Scripture, each man does that which seems good in his own eyes. And again, the LGBTQ movement is not merely satisfied with defining their own lives as they see fit, but are also intent on forcing society, and Christians in particular, to recognize and affirm their choices. Barack Obama's administration has demanded that all publicly funded schools allow students claiming a gender that differs from their biological sex to play for the sports teams of their choice and use the bathroom of their choice, and Canadian Prime Minister Justin Trudeau has announced special legislation for the protection of transgender people from hate, a word that can be quite loosely defined. In 2016, states like South Carolina came under massive pressure from corporations threatening to boycott and remove their businesses for passing laws stipulating that people were required to use the bathroom that matched their biological sex. The same year in Lethbridge, Alberta, a formal investigation was launched after a police officer objected on his private Facebook page to a transgender woman (a biological male) representing "100 Years of Women's Suffrage" in the Alberta legislature. The officer's only objection was that this person could not possibly understand the real struggles of women, such as child-birth and maternity leave. For this, he was labeled "ignorant and hateful."[127]

When our society considers truth to be ignorant and hateful, our society has become one that is increasingly dangerous for Christians. In a contest of liberties that pits the values of the Sexual Revolution against the values of Christianity, sexual liberty always wins, whether it be a baker forced to bake a cake for a lesbian wedding or the life of a pre-born child being violently ended to sustain her mother's lifestyle.

YOU CAN BE CHRISTIAN, OR YOU CAN BE SUCCESSFUL

I always find it fascinating to travel in formerly Communist countries—the combination of decaying Soviet architecture and Western modernity, the resilience of the people, and above all, how in so many cases it was Christianity that helped the oppressed peoples hold onto their families, their cultural heritage, and their hope. There are so many lessons Westerners should learn from how Communism took hold, and how its leaders tried to oppress, disenfranchise, and homogenize the peoples under their rule.

Indeed, there are striking similarities between how the totalitarian Communists of the Eastern Bloc and the Sexual Revolutionaries here in the West attempt to enforce their secular and anti-Christian ideology.

One similarity struck me in Budapest some time ago, when our tour guide stopped on the steps of St. Stephen's Basilica to explain how the Hungarian Communists "dealt with" the Christians. It wasn't that you couldn't be a Christian, she said. You could pray at home, worship at home with your family, even get baptized and go to church. However, you had a choice. "You could either be a Christian," she told us, "or you could be successful." Case in point: Because her family was Christian and she was baptized, her older sister was the first member of their family to be able to attend university, but only after the disintegration of the Soviet Union.

This tactic is very much being utilized by the secular culture warriors here in North America as they seek to enforce their ideologies on everything from sexuality to abortion and euthanasia. We still have freedom of religion in Canada and the United States—we can worship with our families, attend church, and hold whichever views we choose to hold. But what the secularists are attempting to do is to give people a choice in the West: You can be a Christian, or you can be successful. The subtle shift in language by politicians such as Barack Obama—changing "freedom of religion" to "freedom of worship"—is a sign that this is being done very consciously.

One of the easiest ways to push Christians to the margins of society is to slowly but surely implement policies that force them out of traditionally elite professions, such as law and medicine. That is precisely what the cultural enforcers of secularism have been doing—and they're picking up speed. It's not full-out war on Christianity, but death by a thousand cuts.

For example, Ontario's College of Physicians and Surgeons recently tabled a proposal that would force doctors to provide abortions and contraceptives in certain circumstances, and coerce them to refer for them in virtually all. According to LifeSiteNews:

> The proposed policy would compel a physician who refuses a procedure for reasons of conscience to assist the patient in finding a doctor who would provide the procedure. If a referral is not possible, it says, the doctor "must provide care that is urgent or otherwise necessary to prevent imminent harm, suffering, and/or deterioration, even where that care conflicts with their religious or moral beliefs." Released in December, the College's governing council will vote on the policy in June.[128]

If these proposals were passed, Christians would have to consider the fact that the medical establishment would attempt to force them into unethical behaviors, possibly including the destruction of human life. Thanks to this policy many Christians considering medical school could well decide to opt for a field that does not force them into ethical dilemmas. The ultimate goal of keeping Christians out of the medical establishment is furthered.

In other words: "You can be a Christian, or you can be a successful doctor."

The same goes for the legal profession in Canada, with the attack on Christians in the legal community being most publicly manifested in the actions taken against the proposed law school at Trinity Western University. Trinity Western University is, of course, a Christian university, and like many other Christian schools, asks that its students sign a covenant pledging obedience to the biblical view of morality, including on sexuality. Because of this traditional Christian view, the Law Society of British Columbia, the Nova Scotia Barrister's Society, and the Law Society of Upper Canada declared that they would bar any graduates of Trinity Western's proposed law school from practicing law—ironically, because they felt that Trinity Western was not appropriately "inclusive."

Here, at least, Christians in Canada have scored one major victory, when Justice Campbell of the Nova Scotia Supreme Court unceremoniously overturned the Nova Scotia Barrister's Society's decision. According to LifeSiteNews, Campbell wrote:

> In trying to shun TWU students...the law society exceeded its authority. Its mandate to regulate legal practice in Nova Scotia does not include the power to order universities or law schools to change their policies. There is no indication TWU students would be inadequately trained, yet the law society would ban them anyway...If TWU did not exist, the same students holding the same beliefs would be free to obtain law degrees elsewhere.[129]

Indeed. But other organizations in Canada are working hard and fast to make sure that reasonable judges like Justice Campbell do not prevail. Organizations such as one of Trinity Western's most ardent foes, "Legal Leaders for Diversity" (LLD). Although many Christians have never heard of this organization, the policies that LLD seeks to implement in the legal sphere have dramatic consequences. As Ottawa lawyer Albertos Polizogopoulos described the situation:

> The Legal Leaders for Diversity (LLD)… is made up of the heads of the legal departments from more than 70 major corporations. The campaign involves its own form of community covenant by these 70+ corporations (including BMO, Ford, The Globe and Mail and the Edmonton Oilers) to restrict hiring of law firms for their legal work to those who have a commitment to "diversity" and "inclusiveness." The LLD's definition of these words requires approval of same-sex marriage and excludes Christians or others who might have a different opinion.
>
> The LLD publicly opposed TWU's proposed law school on the basis that TWU's Community Covenant is not "inclusive."

> This direct attack on Christian lawyers is meant to create a chilling effect in the legal profession. Lawyers who work for law firms seeking to do business with these corporations will hesitate, and perhaps even be barred from voicing their religious and moral beliefs, or for acting for religious clients in human rights cases dealing with these issues. It's a scary time to be a Christian lawyer in Canada.[130]

In other words? If Legal Leaders for Diversity has their way, you can be Christian, or you can be a successful lawyer.

Across both Canada and the United States, these tactics are being utilized to keep Christians out of many professions. Two of Canada's three main political parties and one of America's two main political parties enforce a pro-abortion status quo. The medical establishment across the continent is under constant pressure to assist or refer for abortions, and Canada's Liberal government actually voted against including conscience protections for healthcare providers in its 2016 euthanasia legislation. It's a clever strategy and a dangerous one, as it gives Christians less and less control over their own futures. If fewer Christians enter politics, our voice in the public square will grow quieter. If fewer Christians enter the field of medicine, we will all suffer. And if organizations like Legal Leaders for Diversity and many others have their way, there will be far fewer Christian lawyers – which means that as Christians increasingly need legal assistance to defend their dwindling religious freedoms, they will have fewer lawyers to rely on. If we do not fight back now, we will soon arrive at the day in North America where we have a choice: We can be Christian, or we can be successful.

THE CHRISTIAN COUNTER-CULTURE

In the midst of all of this, a counter-culture is forming, one buoyed by the unflagging optimism that has so often marked Christian movements. While writers like Peter Hitchens are convinced that Western civilization is in a state of irreversible implosion, others refuse to cede defeat. One of those men is Dr. Robert P. George, a McCormick Professor of Jurisprudence at Princeton University who holds degrees from Swarthmore, Harvard, and Oxford, and has been labeled America's "most influential conservative Christian thinker" by the *New York Times Magazine*. Much of his work has been cited throughout this book, and his positive outlook so interested me that I decided to give him a call. I mentioned the outlook of Peter Hitchens to him, and asked George how he maintained his cheery disposition in spite of growing cultural hostility.

"Peter is an old friend of mine," George replied with a chuckle, "Peter Hitchens and his wife used to live next door to me and my wife when we were young and just starting out in Oxford…he was a young journalist at the time and we had many conversations. He was on the left in those days and had not yet become a Christian so he's made a long journey, but even then it was easy to see the brilliance in him that you see now. [But] I don't think Peter spends a lot of time teaching young people like I do, and when I see young people in my classes and emerging from the university here at Princeton like Sherif Gergis, and Ryan Anderson, and [so on]..some of these names will be known to you, some of them perhaps not, but when I see just these enormous numbers of young, brave, *brilliant*, dedicated, pro-life, pro-marriage, pro-religious liberty people…when I see the sheer numbers, and the brilliance, and the courage, how can you not be lifted up in hope and in confidence? I mean, these people are willing to take on the culture, and they know how to do it. They are armed. They are armed with arguments, they are armed with critical thinking ability, with knowledge, and they're dedicated. They won't be bought off, and they won't be intimidated. I see this all the time, and it's just inspiring for me."

Can you name one situation that has inspired you recently? I asked him. Dr. George's voice got increasingly animated.

"Well, one instance I had recently was bringing together Christian and Jewish young people, devout people on both sides of the Christian-Jewish divide, to discuss their shared convictions," he replied emphatically, "especially their moral convictions, to engage with each other, to learn from each other, to learn about each other's traditions, and to stand together in the great cultural struggles that we're facing! It was a very inspiring thing to watch. I see these friendships developing across the historic lines of religious division and real dedication and genuine fellowship, not just a marriage of convenience. I don't think this has happened in human history—but it's happening now! Now maybe it's happening because people of all the traditional faiths are so embattled, maybe that's why it's happening, but look, the Lord works in mysterious ways, His wonders to perform, and He seems to be performing some wonders now with these young people."

A good reminder. To complete Dr. George's quote from William Cowper's beautiful hymn:

> God moves in a mysterious way
> His wonders to perform;
> He plants His footsteps in the sea
> And rides upon the storm.
>
> Deep in unfathomable mines
> Of never failing skill
> He treasures up His bright designs
> And works His sovereign will.
>
> Ye fearful saints, fresh courage take;
> The clouds ye so much dread
> Are big with mercy and shall break
> In blessings on your head.
>
> Judge not the Lord by feeble sense,
> But trust Him for His grace;
> Behind a frowning providence
> He hides a smiling face.
>
> His purposes will ripen fast,
> Unfolding every hour;
> The bud may have a bitter taste,
> But sweet will be the flower.
>
> Blind unbelief is sure to err
> And scan His work in vain;
> God is His own interpreter,
> And He will make it plain.

Conclusion: The Way Forward

Push back as hard as the age that pushes against you.

—Flannery O'Connor

Say not the struggle nought availeth,
The labour and the wounds are vain,
The enemy faints not, nor faileth,
And as things have been they remain.

If hopes were dupes, fears may be liars;
It may be, in yon smoke concealed,
Your comrades chase e'en now the fliers,
And, but for you, possess the field.

For while the tired waves, vainly breaking
Seem here no painful inch to gain,
Far back through creeks and inlets making,
Comes silent, flooding in, the main.

—Arthur Hugh Clough

While it is not my intention to provide an activist or apologetics handbook, I *do* hope this book will serve as a handbook for activists and apologists. I believe that having a historical and cultural understanding of what has taken place in Western society over the preceding decades is vital to understanding how we have arrived at this point in history and where we must go from here. "To comprehend the history of a thing," the poet Hilaire Belloc once wrote, "is to unlock the mysteries of its present, and more, to disclose the profundities of the future."

With notable exceptions, many Christian communities have found themselves reticent to get involved in the current culture wars.

This is not only apathy, although apathy is certainly prevalent. Nor is it ignorance, although ignorance plays a significant role. One of the primary reasons is a fundamental attitude that runs much deeper. Church-going people are often traditional, conservative people. And here I don't mean those terms in the way that political analysts might use them, to describe specific policy positions. I mean simply that they are people who want to work hard, raise their children, and be left alone.

"Have you ever met a parent of nine kids who was a Democratic activist?" radio show host Dennis Praeger once asked an audience wryly. Everyone laughed. Perhaps not everyone even knew why it was so funny—it was just an absurd thought. Such a parent, everyone presumes, would have better things to do. People like my grandparents, who immigrated virtually penniless to Canada from the Netherlands in 1953, began working the land, and raised eleven children on a farm they built through blood, sweat, toil, and tears. They were too busy raising their children and putting food on the table to trouble themselves with the screechings of feminists and other such activists.

Herein lies the problem the pro-life and pro-family movement has in recruiting conservative people to engage the culture: To such people, there is something fundamentally foreign about "activism." Indeed, the term "conservative activist" itself seems to be something of a contradiction in terms. Small-c conservatives and traditionalists do not want to change the world. They want to live in it and not be bothered.

It's in the very root of the word: "conserve." It is markedly different in temperament from "liberal," which denotes "liberalizing"—*action*. Thus, many suspicious church people find that even the word "activism" carries with it a whiff of liberalism. Ambrose Bierce brilliantly encapsulated the contrast between these two temperaments when he defined a conservative as: "A statesman who is enamored of existing evils, as distinguished from the liberal who wishes to replace them with others."

This brings us to our present unpleasant realization that from a cultural perspective, the traditionalists and conservatives have been thoroughly beaten in the war for the culture. For the most part, we never even showed up. We raised families, built farms and businesses, and attended church functions while secular revolutionaries took over the entertainment industry, the media, academia—and finally, the public education system that now dutifully serves as a conduit for secular "values." Prayer is out, queer theory is in, and many a middle-aged conservative has found occasion recently to splutter his coffee and gape at his newspaper: "How did things *change so fast*?"

They didn't, of course. As we have seen, the Sexual Revolution has been unfolding now for over sixty years. But now, for the first time, people are beginning to wake up and realize that what is happening is not something we can ignore, because very rapidly, it is beginning to happen *to us*. Already, the influences of the entertainment industry and pornography are showing in the youth. Churches across North America are hemorrhaging young people as the public education system dutifully does what it was put in place to do: Plant skepticism, undermine the beliefs of any children from Christian homes, and then send them off to university so that the faculty there can finish the job. It's why enormous numbers of Christians lose their faith during university.

The government too, will no longer leave us alone. As I wrote in Chapter 2, the state has claimed the right to re-educate children into the values of their secular system, and will go to war with parents for the right to do so. In some European countries, children are being taken away from their parents because Christian beliefs could "harm" the children—and some academics are already suggesting that Christianity could, one day, be "treatable" as a backwards pathology. Conservatives want to be left alone to raise their children. The unfortunate fact is that we won't be.

The tables have been turned. Now, it is the secular ideology that is the status quo, having successfully infiltrated and established itself in every major institution. The secularists have achieved a new status quo, and we traditionalists have been left with nothing left to "conserve" in the first place. We can no longer be Neville Chamberlain giving up territory bit-by-bit. We are now the proverbial frog in boiling water, and have to decide how to confront these encroachments to retain the freedoms we need to live as Christians in a society that increasingly holds us in contempt.

How can one be a conservative in a society with nothing left to conserve and everything to fight for? It's a pressing, imminent question that demands our attention. The twofold task of passing our Christian beliefs on to our children and preventing the government from interfering in that process was once easy—we could just live and let live. That was always a questionable strategy, especially as it ignored the massive loss of life through abortion happening in our own towns and cities. Standing up for our pre-born neighbors is not just a "cause," but a biblical command. But now, it is in our self-interest to engage. It is not just the children of others we should be worried about, but our own. We will not have the luxury of raising children the way our parents and grandparents did. It is our responsibility to arm ourselves with tools that will assist us in navigating a hostile future. Chapter by chapter, I would like to offer a few observations and humble suggestions, and I will include more resources in the appendix.

The Sexual Revolution

To many people, the study of history seems a tedious and useless pursuit. But in terms of understanding the cultural moment we find pressing in all around us, an understanding of the history of the Sexual Revolution is absolutely essential. The ideologies of the Sexual Revolution now form the basis of nearly every field of study in academia, and Christian university students often have no idea that what they are learning in education, law, psychology, or anthropology is actually based on the work of Margaret Mead or Dr. Alfred Kinsey. They will in all probability hear arguments made against Christianity based on faulty research and junk science. To know the history of the Sexual Revolution is to have an invaluable context for what is taught in secular universities, and to possesses a greater confidence in the Christian worldview that will not be as easily shaken.

Each summer at the Canadian Centre for Bio-Ethical Reform, I teach a course on the culture wars to dozens of university students and high schoolers. Every time, as I'm speaking, I see shock and realization spread across their faces as many of the things they have been taught click into place. "That makes so much sense!" they tell me. And when the summer ends and they head back to their places of learning, I get messages throughout the year.

"My professor is using Alfred Kinsey to defend sex education. Can you send me your lecture notes?"

"One of my fellow students is citing the Kinsey Reports to attack the Christian view of sexuality. Can you email me the titles of some of your sources?"

"Thank you so much for your course this summer. It helped me understand everything my prof was saying in my mandatory sexuality course!"

These students, armed with the historical and cultural context necessary to understand what they were being taught, were thus prepared to defend their own worldview. In academic institutions often openly hostile to Christian belief, this context provides an invaluable confidence.

Hook-up culture

As I mentioned in the introduction to this book, hook-up culture is now so prevalent that in many cases, it has even permeated Christian communities. In a culture saturated with sex, the idea that sex is a beautiful gift to be enjoyed within the confines of marriage is one that is downright foreign. In Chapter 2, I have tried to highlight what happened to a culture that has rejected the Christian view of sexuality and has instead embraced carnal anarchy. The result speaks for itself: Dozens of new sexually transmitted diseases, the degradation of marriage, and a profound and pervasive unhappiness.

To counter that, Christians must take pains to educate their children on the Christian view of sexuality. Too often, parental discomfort with talking about sexuality has resulted in children learning about sex from friends, films, TV, or even worse, pornography. It is no longer enough to oppose the radical sex education of the secularists while declining to replace it with anything else. Children *will* learn about sex, and the only relevant question parents face is who they would like their children to learn about sex from. It can be from the parents, or it can be from the culture. The choice is ours.

Which brings me to a final, more controversial point: Parents should not send their children to public schools unless they want their children to be effectively re-educated on nearly every matter of importance to Christians, including sexuality. Sending children into an educational system in which they will be taught specifically anti-Christian views for eight hours a day, five days a week, ten months of the year is nearly guaranteeing that their views will be shaped by the ideology of the state. It is simply not realistic to expect that some parental counter-arguments, church services, or catechism classes will be enough to combat what they are hearing on a daily basis. Nearly all statistical evidence shows this to be the case.

I've heard some parents say that their children can be a Christian witness in the public school system. I find that to be dubious at best, and foolish at worst—children are meant to be nurtured and taught, not sent off to be small soldiers in the culture war. That idea strikes me as a modern-day Children's Crusade, and will most likely end in a similar fashion. Private schools, Christian schools, or home-schooling are potential options—but at the end of the day, what is paramount is that Christian parents take responsibility for the education of their children and ensure that they are not being poisoned by a system that stands in opposition to everything they believe.

PORNOGRAPHY AND RAPE CULTURE

Pornography is, without exaggeration, the number one threat to North American families. As I explained in Chapters 3 and 4, pornography is rewiring the brains of millions of people, destroying families, and creating a violent new ideology of sex that is giving rise to something that could be called "rape culture." In nearly every home, portals to pornography in the form of tablets, laptops, and cell phones provide nearly instantaneous access to the vilest filth the human imagination can create.

Porn-proofing the home is a Christian responsibility. Filters should be installed on all devices with Internet access as well as accountability programs, which send a report of your Internet history to a selected accountability partner every week to ensure that porn addictions cannot flourish with the privacy and anonymity the Internet offers. Essential anti-porn tools include Covenant Eyes Internet Accountability and Filtering, which can be accessed at www.covenanteyes.com, Qustodio Family Protection, which can be found at www.qustodio.com, or DNSthingy Filtering, which you can find at www.dnsthingy.com. Pornography is poisonous, and it is stronger than you are. To leave devices unprotected is the equivalent of leaving closets full of pornography about the house under the assumption that no one will ever open the door out of temptation or curiosity.

Again, education is key. Many people, and many Christians, are under the false impression that pornography is more or less harmless. They believe they can view porn casually or even compulsively, and yet enter and sustain healthy relationships and marriages. They believe their minds are impervious to the insidious impact of pornographic images and videos. They must be told the truth. Pornography is not only spiritually deadly; it is physically poisonous. In short: porn wrecks everything. I have seen scores of people quit using pornography after being presented with that evidence. We must make it our business to do so.*

ABORTION

One of the primary reasons Christians sometimes shy away from pro-life outreach is that they are under the illusion that the pro-life case is a complex and difficult one to make. The case against abortion is actually quite simple: Human beings have human rights. Human rights can only logically begin when the human being begins. Science tells us that a living, unique, whole human being begins at fertilization. Thus, abortion is an act of violence that ends the life of a developing human being. Time and time again, I see people change their minds and even cancel abortions after hearing the facts presented in this simple way.

---

* Organizations and resources dedicated to spreading awareness about the porn industry and porn-proofing homes and communities are included in the appendix.

But one of the reasons the culture often doesn't take abortion more seriously is because many Christians don't take abortion very seriously. We say that more than a million babies are being brutally destroyed in North America every year. From a spiritual perspective, let me put it this way: each year, God uses acts of love to bring about irreplaceable children created in His image, children that never existed before and will never exist again. And one by one, day after day, we carve Return To Sender into their tiny corpses and pitch them back into Eternity. And yet, millions of Christians do not seem to care. This sends a powerful message to the rest of the culture. *If abortion is murder,* they wonder, *why don't any of you act like it?*

Everyone has a role to play in the pro-life movement. You can volunteer for crisis pregnancy centres, donate to effective pro-life organizations, and contact your local politicians whenever abortion-related legislation surfaces in the halls of power. Most importantly, you can educate yourself in pro-life apologetics so that you can be an effective ambassador for pre-born children and against abortion.

Showing the reality of abortion is also essential to changing the culture on this issue—it was imagery of the victims that helped sway the people of Great Britain to the cause of abolition during William Wilberforce's time, it was photographs of beleaguered children that turned the American public against the cruel practices of child labor after the Industrial Revolution, and it is the photographic evidence of tiny, shredded children that is most effective in waking people up to the reality that abortion is a cruel injustice. Images have the power to weigh on the consciences of those who see them, and this weight is what often brings about a change in their point of view.*

Euthanasia

Euthanasia has now come to several American states as well as Canada, and many people have been asking how they can resist this new manifestation of the culture of death. First of all, of

* Organizations and resources for learning pro-life apologetics are included in the appendix.

course, organizations seeking to lobby the government against euthanasia and demanding safeguards for vulnerable people deserve the support of all Christians. Even where the public supports euthanasia or so-called "assisted suicide," lobbying can have an incredible effect. In Scotland in 2015, for example, Members of Parliament rejected "assisted suicide" 82-36, in spite of what was perceived as widespread public backing.

Political solutions, however, are tenuous and temporary when public support for euthanasia grows. As a result, it is vitally important that we educate ourselves on these issues so that we can present to our peers the reality of what legal euthanasia actually looks like. The counter-arguments of Christians to the very loud voices shouting for death on demand have been quiet at best and silent at worst. As always, educating ourselves and arming ourselves with the truth is vital to our ability to be effective witnesses in a culture that so rarely hears our point of view.

From a practical perspective, it is also important that Christians support palliative care initiatives and pay careful attention to the care of our disabled and elderly. In a culture that devalues the weak and vulnerable, we must take all precautions to ensure that such people are safe and properly cared for. As euthanasia becomes more prevalent, we must be prepared to respond to increasingly difficult situations.*

Commodity culture and religious liberty

Chapters 7 and 8 pull together the various fronts of the culture war and illustrate the fundamental interconnectedness of hook-up culture, abortion, eugenics, euthanasia, pornography, and the sexual exploitation industries. To understand these connections is to suddenly have a more accurate picture of the enemy that we face and a better understanding of how ideas our culture has adopted are resulting in disturbing and sometimes unforeseen consequences. I found that discovering these connections was enormously helpful in understanding how our trashing of Judeo-

---

* Organizations and resources dealing with euthanasia can be found in the appendix.

Christian principles, one by one, has shredded the moral fabric of our culture, one loose thread at a time.

Chapter 8 specifically deals with the end game of the Sexual Revolutionaries: compulsory acceptance of a variety of sexualities, lifestyles, and radical self-determination. In response, Christians must prepare themselves for inevitable persecution as our legal systems and governments align with the new morality—and against us. We must prepare ourselves to respond by studying apologetics found in books like Albert Mohler's *We Cannot Be Silent* and the brilliant works of Robert P. George. As William Wilberforce wrote centuries ago, "Christianity has been successfully attacked and marginalized… because those who professed belief were unable to defend the faith from attack, even though its attackers' arguments were deeply flawed."

We must also fight every step of the way. A Christian lawyer once commented to me that one of the reasons the secularists have been so successful is that while we simply want to be left alone, secular culture warriors have been engaged in a relentless scorched-earth policy in which they will fight tooth and nail over every tiny point of contention with Christians. Too often, we count the cost and decide that to fight will cost too much money, take too much time, or will be too unpleasant. Too often we lose by forfeit. As the amount of space our secular society allots to us shrinks and we find ourselves backed into our churches and our homes, we will have to rethink this strategy. Rev. Douglas Wilson commented wryly on this habit on his blog in 2015:

> Whenever we get to that elusive and ever-receding "hill to die on," we will discover, upon our arrival there, that it only looked like a hill to die on from a distance. Up close, when the possible dying is also up close, it kind of looks like every other hill. All of a sudden it looks like a hill to stay alive on, covered over with topsoil that looks suspiciously like common ground. So it turns out that surrendering hills is not the best way to train for defending the most important ones. Retreat is habit-forming.[131]

Over the preceding decades, Christians have learned the art of surrender. Forced into a corner, we can only hope this attitude will change.*

A FINAL THOUGHT

Above all, of course, we must pray. Our culture has rejected God, and in fighting the symptoms of that rejection, we cannot forget the disease itself. "Pray like everything depends on God," Augustine of Hippo instructed, "Work like everything depends on you."

William Wilberforce, that great Christian reformer, had words for Christians fighting uphill battles in a hostile culture. "Is it not the great end of religion, and, in particular, the glory of Christianity," he wrote, "to extinguish the malignant passions; to curb the violence, to control the appetites, and to smooth the asperities of man; to make us compassionate and kind, and forgiving one to another; to make us good husbands, good fathers, good friends; and to render us active and useful in the discharge of the relative social and civil duties?"

To conclude, I would like to echo the sentiments of Abraham Lincoln in the greatest speech in American history: "With malice toward none, with charity for all, with firmness in the right as God gives us to see the right, let us strive on to finish the work we are in, to bind up the nation's wounds, to care for him who shall have borne the battle and for his widow and his orphan, to do all which may achieve and cherish a just and lasting peace among ourselves and with all nations."

---

* Organizations and resources dealing with commodity culture and religious liberty can be found in the appendix.

Appendix

A list of organizations and resources the reader may find helpful:

Pornography

Strength To Fight (www.strengthtofight.ca) is a Canadian non-profit organization based out of Ottawa focused on educating families, churches, and communities on the dangers of pornography and how to fight them. Featuring a team of experienced speakers, they are the only organization in Canada focused exclusively on combatting pornography.

Covenant Eyes (www.covenanteyes.com) is an essential filtering and accountability service featuring a team of tech experts well-equipped to help you porn-proof your home or your business. They also feature regular practical blog posts, release recent statistics on pornography, and provide free-of-charge e-books such as *Hope After Porn, Porn and Your Husband, Fight Porn In Your Church,* and many others.

Qustodio (www.qustodio.com) is an incredibly effective parental control software that allows parents to filter, track, and monitor the phones of their children. It features time limits for Internet usage, call blocking options, and social media monitoring. For concerned parents, this software is essential.

DNSthingy (www.dnsthingy.com) is another layer of protection for families seeking to porn-proof their homes, featuring, according to their website, "Customized white lists, black lists, rainbow lists and all of the benefits of OpenDNS you can block adult content; unwanted sites, malware and phishing to protect your computer from potentially harmful content."

Fight the New Drug (www.fightthenewdrug.org) is an American non-profit focused on raising awareness and creating an international youth movement to oppose porn use and the porn industry. Featuring the well-known "Porn Kills Love" t-shirts and other swag, Fight the New Drug has amassed an enormous social media following in a very short amount of time and has proven incredibly effective at disseminating information about the negative impacts of pornography.

Note: I would not advise readers to purchase many of the resources I used to write chapters 3 and 4. The graphic and explicit descriptions of pornography and the revelations of what goes on within the porn industry by people like Dr. Gail Dines were nothing short of nauseating, and one of my goals with this book was to provide people with the truth they need to hear without forcing them to wade through the same dark, poisonous material I had to read.

ABORTION

The Canadian Centre for Bio-Ethical Reform (www.endthekilling.ca) is the largest educational pro-life organization in Canada, reaching millions of Canadians with the truth about abortion each year. Featuring a variety of internships throughout the year, CCBR trains dozens of young people to engage the culture on abortion and utilize abortion victim photography and effective apologetics to impact the culture in profound ways.

The Center for Bio-Ethical Reform (www.abortionno.org) is an American-based organization which engages in pro-life outreach through the use of abortion victim photography. Most of the abortion victim photography the pro-life movement utilizes was obtained by the founder of CBR, Gregg Cunningham.

We Need A Law (www.weneedalaw.ca) is a Canadian pro-life lobbying organization seeking to pass laws restricting abortion on both the provincial and federal level.

Life Training Institute (www.prolifetraining.com) is an organization "established in 2004 to challenge and equip pro-life advocates to persuasively defend their views in the public square."

Created Equal (www.createdequal.org) is a pro-life organization based out of Columbus, Ohio that utilizes abortion victim photography and pro-life apologetics to impact the culture.

The Grantham Collection (www.abortioninstruments.com) is a collection of abortion tools and abortion victim photography that details the barbarism of the abortion industry in excruciating detail.

Images of Abortion (www.imagesofabortion.com) is a collection of abortion victim photography and a project of Dr. Monica Miller and Citizens for a Pro-Life Society.

Operation Rescue (www.operationrescue.org) is a pro-life activist organization based out of Wichita, Kansas, and located in a former abortion clinic. Run by Troy Newman and Cheryl Sullenger, they focus on exposing what is going on within the abortion industry and utilizing undercover tactics to shut down abortion clinics across the United States.

Note: Invaluable books on pro-life apologetics have been cited for reference in the footnotes of this book.

Euthanasia

Euthanasia Prevention Coalition (www.epcc.ca) is a Canadian-based organization which lobbies against mercy killing and seeks to implement legal protections for vulnerable people.

The Association for Reformed Political Action, or ARPA (www.arpacanada.ca) is a Canadian organization that lobbies the government on behalf of Christians, opposing euthanasia, abortion, and threats to religious liberty.

Religious Liberty

The Thomas More Society (www.thomasmoresociety.org) is an US-based "not-for-profit, national public interest law firm dedicated to restoring respect in law for life, family, and religious liberty.)

Alliance Defending Freedom (www.adflegal.org) is an American Christian non-profit organization with the stated goal of "defending the right to hear and speak the Truth through strategy, training, funding, and litigation."

The Justice Centre for Constitutional Freedoms (www.jccf.ca) is a Canadian non-profit focused on the protection of religious liberty.

Acknowledgements

To my editors—without my wife Charmaine poring over the manuscript for countless hours and fighting with me to make every sentence better, this book would not exist. My colleague Alex Vande Bruinhorst also spent more hours than I can count painstakingly searching the book for any mistakes and reading and rereading to ensure that the narrative flowed. The feedback of Blaise Alleyne and Cana Donovan was also much appreciated.

To Gerrit Van Dorland, who took the time to put his artistic skills to work designing a brilliant cover.

To Nick and Maaike Rosendal, who are precious friends and more essential to the pro-life movement than most people will ever know.

To Nicholas McLeod, who was there with me from the very beginning. His brilliant strategic mind has transformed the front lines of pro-life activism in Canada.

To my colleagues at the Canadian Centre for Bio-Ethical Reform, who supported me through months of part-time writing and offered their feedback and encouragement, and who take to the front lines of the culture war every single day—Devorah Gilman, Justina Van Maren, Caroline Slingerland, Pieter Bos, Cameron Cote, Dan Zeleny, Rachel Dalcin, Yvonne Boon, Jeremy Hoogheim, Irene de Souza, Kianna Owen, Sophia Vandersluis, Emily Ryznar, Caleb VanderWeide, Janelle Van Hierden, Brittany Van de Bruinhorst, Rosalyn DeHaan, Oriyana Hrycyshyn, Christine De Baets, Alex Sibiga, Wilma Zekveld, Alanna Gomez, Carol Crosson, and Siobhan McLeod.

To Ted Byfield, a journalist and writer I admired from afar as I grew up, and did me the honor of writing the foreword for this book.

To Rev. Cornelius Sonnevelt, who has a heart for pre-born children and always encouraged us to stay the course.

To my family, for whom I am more grateful than I will ever be able to express—Dad, Mom, Justina and Ben, Joel, Janelle and Nick, and my princess Jessalyn. Thank you for everything.

To my Tante Marianne Luteyn, who spent hours on the phone with me through the early chapters of this book, offering valuable advice and feedback.

To the supporters of the pro-life movement, including many generous and supportive friends and family members, who keep pro-life activists on the front lines with their generous assistance. What we do would not be possible without them.

To my friend Steffan, who commented after reading the first draft, "It's like reliving 98% of our discussions in print." To the friends who challenged me, debated me, and spent long evenings in intellectual conversation on these issues with me over the past five years and beyond, such as Edward W., Jojo Ruba, Daniel Gilman, Dr. Alexander Moens, Ted Gerk, William VanderWeide, Cameron Wilson, and J.J. McCullough, among others.

To Paul Broughton and the team at Life Cycle, for accepting this manuscript and working so hard to get it published.

To Troy Newman and Monica Miller, who wrote kind and generous endorsements of this book.

To the many brave and brilliant warriors I have met in the pro-life and pro-family movement over the past years, thank you for teaching me so much, answering thousands of questions, and inspiring me to follow your example.

Soli Deo Gloria.

About the Author

Jonathon Van Maren is a pro-life activist, columnist, radio host, and public speaker. His writings have been translated into more than six languages and published in the *National Post*, the *Jewish Independent*, the *Hamilton Spectator*, the *Reformed Perspective Magazine*, LifeNews, and many other places. He also writes a weekly culture column for LifeSiteNews.com. His writing has garnered him an award from the Jewish organization B'nai Brith for combatting anti-Semitism in print.

Jonathon's commentary has been featured on CTV Primetime, Global News, EWTN, and the CBC as well as dozens of radio stations and news outlets in both Canada and the United States. He speaks on a wide range of cultural topics in both Canada and the United States at universities, high schools, churches, and other functions. Some of these topics include abortion, pornography, the Sexual Revolution, and euthanasia.

Jonathon graduated from Simon Fraser University in 2010 with a Bachelor of Arts Degree in History. He is the communications director for the Canadian Centre for Bio-Ethical Reform.

Learn more at **www.thebridgehead.ca**, **www.endthekilling.ca**, and **www.lifesitenews.com/blogs/author/jonathon-van-maren**

Endnotes

Chapter 1

1 Statistics Canada, "Canadians attend weekly religious services less than 20 years ago," www.statcan.gc.ca, December 21, 2008, accessed May 30, 2016, http://www.statcan.gc.ca/pub/89-630-x/2008001/article/10650-eng.htm

2 Church Leaders, "Statistics Don't Tell The Whole Story When It Comes To Church Attendance," www.churchleaders.com, accessed May 30, 2016, http://www.churchleaders.com/pastors/pastor-articles/170739-statistics-don-t-tell-the-whole-story-when-it-comes-to-church-attendance.html

3 Ross Amy, Paul Bunner, Colman Byfield, Link Byfield, Virginia Byfield et al, *The High Tide and the Turn,* (Edmonton: The Society to Record and Explore Christian History, 2013), 64

4 Ibid.

5 John Horgan, "Margaret Mead's bashers owe her an apology," *Scientific American,* October 25, 2010, accessed May 2, 2016, http://blogs.scientificamerican.com/cross-check/margaret-meads-bashers-owe-her-an-apology/

6 Paul Shankman, The Trashing of Margaret Mead: Anatomy of an Anthropological Controversy (Wisconsin: University of Wisconsin Press, 2009), 86.

7 Ross Amy, Paul Bunner, Colman Byfield, Link Byfield, Virginia Byfield et al, *The High Tide and the Turn,* (Edmonton: The Society to Record and Explore Christian History, 2013), 69.

8 "Manners and Morals: How to Stop Gin Rummy," *TIME* (March 1, 1948), 16.

9 Richard Rhotes, "Father of the Sexual Revolution, *New York Times* (New York, NY), November 2, 1997.

10 Judith Reisman, Sex, Lies and Kinsey, *Whistleblower Magazine,* July, 2002.

11 Ibid.

12 Ibid.

13 Christopher Turner, "Hugh Hefner in six volumes," *The Guardian*, July 17, 2010, accessed May 2, 2016, http://www.theguardian.com/books/2010/jul/17/hugh-hefner-playboy-biography

14 Ibid.

15 David Frum, *How We Got Here: The 70's: The Decade That Brought You Modern Life—For Better or Worse,* (USA: Random House, 2000), 190-191.

16 Dr. Judith A. Reisman and Edward W. Eichel, *Kinsey, Sex and Fraud: The Indoctrination of a People,* (Louisiana: Huntington House Publishers, 1990), 84.

17 Rose Eveleth, "The Bikini's Inventor Guessed How Much It Would Horrify The Public," *Smithsonian Mag*, July 5, 2013, accessed May 2, 2016, http://www.smithsonianmag.com/smart-news/the-bikinis-inventor-guessed-how-much-it-would-horrify-the-public-6914887/?no-ist

18 Pamela Paul, *Pornified: How Pornography is Damaging Our Lives, Our Relationships, and our Families,* (New York: Holt Paperbacks, 2006), 50.

19 Allan Bloom, *The Closing of the American Mind,* (New York: Simon and Schuster, 1987), 74-75.

Chapter 2

20 Kathleen A. Bogle, *Hooking Up: Sex, Dating, and Relationships on Campus,* (New York: New York University Press, 2008), 21.

21 Ibid., 25.

22 Jacques Gallant, "Doctor sues mother of his child for emotional damages," *Toronto Star*, January 19, 2016, accessed May 2, 2016, http://www.thestar.com/news/gta/2016/01/16/doctor-sues-mother-of-his-child-for-emotional-damages.html

23 Nathan Harden, *Sex and God at Yale,* (New York: St. Martin's Press, 2012), 11.

24 Ibid., 130.

25 Hanna Rosin, *The End of Men and the Rise of Women* (New York: Riverhead Books, 2013), 21.

26 Bogle, *Hooking Up*, 37.

27 Peter Jon Mitchell, "Almost 90% of teens hope to get married. Sex ed should reflect this," *National Post*, July 16, 2015, accessed May 2, 2016

28 "Reported STDs in the United States 2014 National Data for Chlamydia, Gonorrhea, and Syphilis," Center for Disease Control (Atlanta: 2014), accessed May 2, 2016, http://www.cdc.gov/nchhstp/newsroom/docs/factsheets/std-trends-508.pdf

29 "The Chief Public Health Officer's Report on the State of Public Health in Canada, 2013: Infectious Disease—The Never-Ending Threat," Public Health Agency of Canada (Canada: 2013), accessed May 2, 2016, http://www.phac-aspc.gc.ca/cphorsphc-respcacsp/2013/sti-its-eng.php

30 Ibid.

31 "The HIV/AIDS Epidemic in the United States," The Henry J. Kaiser Family Foundation (California: 2014), accessed May 2, 2016, http://kff.org/hivaids/fact-sheet/the-hivaids-epidemic-in-the-united-states/

32 Bahar Gholipour, "Hidden STD Epidemic: 110 Million Infections in the US," *Live Science*, October 6, 2014, accessed May 2, 2016

33 Amy Desai, J.D., "How Could Divorce Affect My Kids?", accessed May 2, 2016, http://www.focusonthefamily.com/marriage/divorce-and-infidelity/should-i-get-a-divorce/how-could-divorce-affect-my-kids

34 Ibid.

35 Derek Thompson, "The Death (and Life) of Marriage in America," *The Atlantic*, February 2, 2012, accessed May 2, 2016.

36 "Family Life-Divorce," Government of Canada (Canada: 2011), accessed May 2, 2016, http://well-being.esdc.gc.ca/misme-iowb/.3ndic.1t.4r@-eng.jsp?iid=76

37 "Family Life-Marriage," Government of Canada (Canada: 2011), accessed May 2, 2016, http://well-being.esdc.gc.ca/misme-iowb/.3ndic.1t.4r@-eng.jsp?iid=76

Chapter 3

38 Active Healthy Kids, "Report Card on Sedentary Behaviors," www.activehealthykids.ca/reportcard/sedentarybehaviors.aspx, last accessed April 30, 2015

39 Covenant Eyes, *Pornography Statistics: 250+ facts, quotes, and statistics about pornography use,* (Michigan: Covenant Eyes, 2014)

40 Naomi Wolf, "The Porn Myth," *New York Mag*, October 20, 2003, accessed May 3, 2016, http://nymag.com/nymetro/news/trends/n_9437/

41 Catherine Briggs, "Porn use can lead to divorce: study," LifeSiteNews.com, June 9, 2014, last accessed May 3, 2016, https://www.lifesitenews.com/news/porn-use-can-lead-to-divorce-study

42 Covenant Eyes, *Pornography Statistics, 2014.*

43 Anonymous, "A letter to my ex-husband, who preferred pornography to me," *The Guardian*, June 13, 2015, accessed May 3, 2016, http://www.theguardian.com/lifeandstyle/2015/jun/13/a-letter-to-my-ex-husband-who-preferred-pornography-to-me

44 Covenant Eyes, *Pornography Statistics, 2014.*

45 Pamela Paul, *Pornified: How Pornography Is Damaging Our Lives, Our Relationships, and Our Families,* (New York: Holt Paperbacks, 2005), 13.

46 Ibid, 10.

47 Ibid, 9.

48 Ibid, 133.

49 Covenant Eyes, *Pornography Statistics, 2014.*

50 Covenant Eyes, *Pornography Statistics: 250+ facts, quotes, and statistics about pornography use,* (Michigan: Covenant Eyes, 2015), accessed May 3, 2016, http://www.covenanteyes.com/pornstats/

51 Annalisa Barbieri, "You don't know what sexting is?" *The Guardian,* August 7, 2009, accessed May 3, 2016.

52 Covenant Eyes, *Pornography Statistics, 2014.*

53 Dr. Gail Dines, *Pornland: How Porn Has Hijacked Our Sexuality*, (Boston: Beacon Press, 2010), 22.

54 Christine Dhanagom, "Porn numbs body's response to sexual pleasure: Psychology Today," LifeSiteNews.com, October 20, 2011, accessed May 3, 2016, https://www.lifesitenews.com/news/porn-numbs-bodys-response-to-sexual-pleasure-psychology-today

55 Matt Fradd, "Neuroscience has proved that porn is literally making men's brains more childish," LifeSiteNews.com, January 14, 2015, accessed May 3, 2016, https://www.lifesitenews.com/blogs/how-neuroscience-has-proved-that-porn-is-literally-making-mens-brains-more

CHAPTER 4

56 Covenant Eyes, *Pornography Statistics: 250+ facts, quotes, and statistics about pornography use*, (Michigan: Covenant Eyes, 2014).

57 Ben Johnson, "'Empowering'? Video shows Duke pornstar and 'feminist' being choked, degraded, and abused," LifeSiteNews.com, March 20, 2014, accessed on May 3, 2016, https://www.lifesitenews.com/news/empowering-video-shows-duke-pornstar-and-feminist-being-choked-degraded-and

58 Dr. Mary Anne Layden, "Pornography and Violence: A New Look at the Research," in *The Social Costs of Pornography*, ed. James R. Stoner and Donna M. Hughes, (Princeton: The Witherspoon Institute, 2010), 60.

59 Berkman Center for Internet Society at Harvard Law School, "Violence Against Women on the Internet," accessed on May 3, 2016, http://cyber.law.harvard.edu/vaw02/mod2-6.htm

60 Covenant Eyes, *Pornography Statistics, 2014.*

61 Jonathon Van Maren, "If you find this filthy book in your home, burn it," LifeSiteNews.com, July 28, 2014, accessed on May 3, 2016, https://www.lifesitenews.com/blogs/if-you-find-this-filthy-book-in-your-home-burn-it

62 Amy E. Bonomi, Lauren E. Altenburger, and Nicole L. Walton, "'Double Crap!' Abuse and Harmed Identity in *Fifty Shades of Grey*," *Journal of Women's Health* Volume 22, (2013): 1.

63 Alison Flood, "Fifty Shades of Grey condemned as 'manual for torture,'" *The Guardian*, August 24, 2012, accessed May 3, 2016, http://www.theguardian.com/books/2012/aug/24/fifty-shades-grey-domestic-violence-campaigners

64 Tracy Clark-Flory, "When Safe Words Are Ignored, Salon.com, January 28, 2012, accessed May 3, 2016, http://www.salon.com/2012/01/29/real_abuse_in_bdsm/

65 Kevin Donovan, "CBC Fires Jian Ghomeshi Over Sex Allegations," *Toronto Star*, January 29, 2016, accessed May 3, 2016, https://www.thestar.com/news/canada/2014/10/26/cbc_fires_jian_ghomeshi_over_sex_allegations.html

66 Allison Pearson, "Pornography has changed the landscape of adolescence beyond all recognition," *The Telegraph*, April 22, 2015, accessed May 3, 2016, http://www.telegraph.co.uk/women/mother-tongue/11554595/Pornography-has-changed-the-landscape-of-adolescence-beyond-all-recognition.html

67 Ibid.

68 Ibid.

69 Hayden Smith, "Porn 'drives youngsters to violence during sex," *Metro News*, October 8, 2013, accessed May 3, 2016, http://metro.co.uk/2013/10/08/porn-drives-youngsters-to-violence-during-sex-4138086/

70 Jonathon Van Maren, "This former porn star is exposing porn's secrets: and it should make you very, very uncomfortable," LifeSiteNews.com, April 7, 2015, accessed May 3, 2016, https://www.lifesitenews.com/blogs/former-porn-star-porn-was-the-worst-darkest-thing-ive-ever-been-involved-in

Chapter 5

71 George Grant, *Third Time Around: A History of the Pro-Life Movement from the First Century to the Present*, (Tennessee: Wolgemuth & Hyatt Publishers, Inc., 1991), 12.

72 Ibid, 21.

73 Ibid, 27.

74 Ibid, 55-56.

75 Helen Alvare, Greg Pfundstein, and Ryan T. Anderson, "The Lazy Slander of the Pro-Life Cause," *The Public Discourse*, January 17, 2011, accessed May 3, 2016, http://www.thepublicdiscourse.com/2011/01/2380/

76 Daniel K. Williams, *Defenders of the Unborn: The Pro-Life Movement before Roe v. Wade*, (New York: Oxford University Press, 2016), 11.

77 Paul Tuns, "Why the Abortion Law was Changed," *The Interim*, (Toronto: ON), April 1, 2009.

78 *Doe v. Bolton*, 1973.

79 Dr. Bernard N. Nathanson, *The Hand of God: A Journey from Death to Life by the Abortion Doctor Who Changed His Mind*, (Toronto: Life Cycle Books, 1996), 118-119.

80 David Kupelian, *The Marketing of Evil*, (USA: WND Books, 2005), 192.

81 Ibid, 190.

82 Ibid, 191.

83 Pro-Life Action League, "Former Abortion Clinic Owner Carol Everett," *Prolifeaction.org*, accessed May 3, 2016, http://prolifeaction.org/providers/everett.php

84 Sarah Terzo, "Looking Back: Jill Stanek exposed live birth abortions at Illinois hospital," *Live Action News*, July 25, 2015, accessed May 3, 2016, http://liveactionnews.org/looking-back-jill-stanek-exposed-live-birth-abortions-illinois-hospital/

85 Ibid.

86 Ibid.

87 CBC News, "Infanticide conviction nets Alberta woman suspended sentence," September 9, 2011, accessed May 3, 2016, http://www.cbc.ca/news/canada/edmonton/infanticide-conviction-nets-alberta-woman-suspended-sentence-1.991189

88 Steve Weatherbe, "Babies left to die? 182 children born alive, then died, after failed abortions in 2013-14: StatsCan," LifeSiteNews, April 14, 2015, https://www.lifesitenews.com/news/babies-left-to-die-182-children-born-alive-then-died-after-failed-abortions

89 Mark Crutcher, "The Marketing of Aborted Baby Parts," Life Dynamics, March 8, 2000, accessed March 3, 2016, https://lifedynamics.com/busted-the-abortion-industry/bad-medicine/baby-body-parts-for-sale/

90 Sarah Kliff, "Why young voters are lukewarm on abortion rights," Newsweek, April 15, 2010, accessed May 3, 2016, http://www.newsweek.com/why-young-voters-are-lukewarm-abortion-rights-70311

Chapter 6

91 Simon Caldwell, "Elderly couple to die together by assisted suicide even though they are not ill," *Daily Mail*, September 26, 2014, accessed May 3, 2016, http://www.dailymail.co.uk/news/article-2770249/Healthy-OAP-couple-die-assisted-suicide-Husband-wife-support-three-children.html

92 Charles Darwin, *The Descent of Man and Selection in Relation to Sex*, (London: John Murray, 1882), 133.

93 Link Byfield, Virginia Byfield, Ric Dolphin, D'Arcy Jenish, Thomas McFeely et al, *Unto the Ends of the Earth*, (Edmonton: The Society to Record and Explore Christian History, 2012), 242.

94 Ibid, 254.

95 Ibid, 255-256.

96 Ibid, 258-259.

97 Simon Caldwell, "Doctors administered lethal injection to blind Dutch woman," *Daily Mail*, October 7, 2013, accessed May 3, 2016, http://www.dailymail.co.uk/news/article-2448611/Blind-Dutch-woman-euthanised-loss-sight.html?printingPage=true

98 Alex Schadenberg, "Dutch health minister: 42 psychiatric euthanasia deaths in 2013," Euthanasia Prevention Coalition, February 11, 2014, accessed May 3, 2016, http://alexschadenberg.blogspot.ca/2014/02/dutch-health-minister-45-psychiatric.html

99 Jeanne Smits, "There were 4,829 cases of euthanasia in the Netherlands in 2013," LifeSiteNews.com, October 1, 2014, accessed on May 3, 2016, https://www.lifesitenews.com/news/there-were-4829-cases-of-euthanasia-in-the-netherlands-in-2013

100 Daily Mail Reporter, "Mobile Death squads to kill sick and elderly in their own homes leads to surge in suicide rates in the Netherlands," *Daily Mail*, September 24, 2013, accessed May 3, 2016, http://www.dailymail.co.uk/news/article-2430479/One-thirty-deaths-Holland-euthanasia-choosing-end-lives-cancer.html

101 D. Van Raemdonck, G.M. Verleden, L. Dupont et al, "Initial experience with transplantation of lungs recovered from donors after euthanasia," *Applied Cardiopulmonary Pathophysiology*, Volume 15, (2011), 38

102 Wesley J. Smith, "Euthanasia By Organ Harvesting," *First Things*, April 1, 2016, accessed May 3, 2016, http://www.firstthings.com/web-exclusives/2016/04/euthanasia-by-organ-harvesting

103 Robert Carle, "Give Me Liberty and Give Me Death: Belgium's Brave New Euthanasia Regime," *The Public Discourse*, September 8, 2015, accessed May 3, 2016, http://www.thepublicdiscourse.com/2015/09/15355/

104 Wesley J. Smith, "Pushing Infanticide, *The Center for Bio-Ethics and Culture Network*, February 20,2008, accessed May 3, 2016, http://www.discovery.org/a/4477

Chapter 7

105 *The Georgia Straight*, "Joyce Arthur", YouTube video, 1:54. Uploaded June 10, 2011. https://www.youtube.com/watch?v=MHab4-aFUdw

106 Jonathon Van Maren, "Feminism's self-defeating about-face on porn," LifeSiteNews.com, January 26, 2015, accessed May 3, 2016, https://www.lifesitenews.com/blogs/fighting-porn-isnt-anti-sex-its-profoundly-pro-sex-and-pro-woman

107 Robert P. George and Christopher Tollefsen, *Embryo: A Defense of Human Life*, (New York: Doubleday, 2008), 9.

108 Ibid, 9-10.

109 Thaddeus M. Baklinksi, "New Study Confirms Overwhelming Death Rate of Embryos," LifeSiteNews.com, October 26, 2010, accessed May 3, 2016, https://www.lifesitenews.com/news/new-study-confirms-overwhelming-death-rate-of-ivf-human-embryos

110 Lindsey Bever, "'I am pro-life!': A surrogate mother's stand against 'reducing' her triplets," *Washington Post*, January 7, 2016, accessed May 3, 2016, https://www.washingtonpost.com/news/morning-mix/wp/2016/01/07/i-am-not-having-an-abortion-a-surrogate-mothers-stand-against-reducing-her-triplets/

111 Jaqueline Mroz, "One Sperm Donor, 150 Offspring," *New York Times*, September 5, 2011, accessed May 3, 2016, http://www.nytimes.com/2011/09/06/health/06donor.html?_r=2

112 Jonathon Van Maren, "Porn is super-empowering: Just ask the Duke University porn star," LifeSiteNews.com, September 22, 2014, accessed May 3, 2016

Chapter 8

113 R. Albert Mohler, Jr., *We Cannot Be Silent*, (Tennessee: Nelson Books, 2015), 120.

114 Ibid, 33-34.

115 Ibid, 37.

116 Ross Amy, Paul Bunner, Colman Byfield, Link Byfield, Virginia Byfield et al, *The High Tide and the Turn*, (Edmonton: The Society to Record and Explore Christian History, 2013), 242-243.

117 Mohler, Jr., *We Cannot Be Silent*, 39.

118 Ibid, 37-38.

119 The Onion, "Gay-Pride Parade Sets Mainstream Acceptance Of Gays Back 50 Years," www.theonion.com, April 25, 2001, accessed May 30, 2016, http://www.theonion.com/article/gay-pride-parade-sets-mainstream-acceptance-of-gay-351

120 Gallup, "Americans Greatly Overestimate Percent Gay, Lesbian in U.S.," www.gallup.com, May 21, 2015, accessed May 30, 2016, http://www.gallup.com/poll/183383/americans-greatly-overestimate-percent-gay-lesbian.aspx

121 Collider, "GLAAD Report Shows Hollywood Studios Are Failing In Terms of LGBT Visibility," www.collider.com, May 2, 2016, accessed May 30, 2016, http://collider.com/glaad-report-disney-paramount/

122 The Telegraph, "Straight men who watch porn 'more likely to support gay marriage,'" www.thetelegraph.co.uk, February 5, 2013, accessed May 30, 2016, http://www.telegraph.co.uk/women/sex/9849619/Gay-marriage-support-more-likely-from-straight-men-who-watch-porn.html

123 Mohler, Jr., *We Cannot Be Silent*, 123.

124 Ibid, 127.

125 Rod Dreher, "The Next Culture War Front," www.americanconservative.com, December 14, 2015, http://www.theamericanconservative.com/dreher/the-next-culture-war-front-chai-feldblum-jill-soloway/

126 Mohler, Jr., *We Cannot Be Silent*, 70.

127 Matt Battochio, "Investigation launched after Lethbridge officer's post about transgender woman," www.globalnews.ca, April 22, 2016, http://globalnews.ca/news/2655051/trans-women-are-women-period-transgender-woman-fires-back-after-lethbridge-officers-post/

128 Jonathon Van Maren, "You can be Christian, or you can be successful: how the leftists are working (successfully) to squeeze us out," LifeSiteNews.com, February 11, 2016, https://www.lifesitenews.com/blogs/you-can-be-christian-or-you-can-be-successful-how-leftists-are-successfully

129 Lea Singh, "Nova Scotia Court exposes anti-Christian prejudice of the elite," LifeSiteNews.com, February 2, 2015, https://www.lifesitenews.com/opinion/nova-scotia-court-exposes-anti-christian-prejudice-of-legal-elite

130 Albertos Polizogopoulos, "Christian Lawyers and Doctors Need Not Apply," January 9, 2015, Cardus.ca, https://www.cardus.ca/blog/2015/01/christian-lawyers-and-doctors-need-not-apply

Conclusion

131 Douglas Wilson, "In Which I Paint With Some Bright Yellows," September 2, 2015, Blog and Mablog, https://dougwils.com/s7-engaging-the-culture/in-which-i-paint-with-some-bright-yellows.html